After the Dream Comes True

After the Dream Comes True

POST-ADOPTION SUPPORT *for* CHRISTIAN FAMILIES

MICHELLE GARDNER

Pleasant Word

Unless otherwise noted, all Scriptures are taken from the Holy Bible, New International Version, Copyright © 1973, 1978, 1984 by the International Bible Society. Used by permission of Zondervan Publishing House. The "niv" and "New International Version" trademarks are registered in the United States Patent and Trademark Office by International Bible Society.

Scripture references marked kjv are taken from the King James Version of the Bible.

Scripture references marked nasb are taken from the New American Standard Bible, © 1960, 1963, 1968, 1971, 1972, 1973, 1975, 1977 by The Lockman Foundation. Used by permission.

ISBN 1-4141-0267-4
Library of Congress Catalog Card Number: 2004096525

Dedicated to all the children who hope that the next
family to walk through the door is theirs.

Table of Contents

Preface 9

Introduction 13

Part One: Looking At Our Hearts

Chapter 1: Emotions That Might Surprise You 21

Chapter 2: Why You Got Involved with Adoption 29

Chapter 3: Is God Good? 39

Part Two: Looking At Our Homes

Chapter 4: Meeting Your Child and Time Away
    From Home 47

Chapter 5: First Days At Home 59

Chapter 6: Medical Issues 75

Chapter 7: Practical Questions You'll Need to
    Consider 81

Chapter 8: Birthparent Issues 93

Chapter 9: Setting Boundaries and Establishing
    Routines 105
Chapter 10: School Issues 115
Chapter 11: Spiritual Development 129
Chapter 12: Life as an Adoptive Family 133
Chapter 13: Issues Affecting Different Ages 147
Chapter 14: Keeping Your Child's Cultural
    Heritage 163
Chapter 15: Sibling Issues 167

Part Three: Looking at the Future

Chapter 16: If the Dream Becomes a Nightmare 171
Chapter 17: Support Groups 185
Chapter 18: Ready to Adopt Again? 189

Conclusion 199
Appendix 201

Preface

You've done it. After months or even years of prayers, dreams and effort your child is finally home. Now it's time for happily ever after. And yet the days and months ahead will quite likely stretch you in ways you aren't expecting. I'd like to help you anticipate some of these challenges and give you tools to help you cope. Above all I want to remind you that the Lord brought this precious child into your life. You're in for an exciting adventure as His plan for your family unfolds!

Adoption is becoming rather trendy in Christian circles. Several Christian entertainers have adopted recently, and magazine articles and radio shows have been devoted to their stories. Giving exposure to the need for adoption is a good thing. I'm concerned, however, that many families hear these stories, are gripped by the massive need for families for children, and eagerly begin to pursue an adoption without understanding the reality of how it will affect their family.

I hear from many, many families while they are awaiting their child's arrival. Their whole life is focused on bringing their child home. They count the days and count their money, over and over, hoping the days will go by fast and the money will leak out slowly. They are sure this is the most wonderful thing that has ever happened to them.

Often I hear from the same families two weeks after their child has arrived home. Too often, gone is the excitement and joy as the family deals with the reality of assimilating a new child into their home. They want instant bonding with their new child. They wonder how to handle the challenges of daily life. In the saddest cases, the parents wonder if they made a big mistake and whether they should have the child removed from their home.

Of course this isn't always the case. Many families adjust very well, though there are always challenges. As I've pondered what makes the difference for families, it's apparent that the family's preparation and expectations matter significantly. When families are aware of many of the normal issues they will face and think through how they plan to handle things, the challenges will still present themselves but the family is often able to deal with them more easily.

I have written this book to encourage you through the first year of life as an adoptive family. Please remember that many of these issues are controversial, with people having strong opinions from different perspectives. I will help you consider options, but ultimately of course you need to make your own decisions and not feel you owe people an explanation for the decisions you made.

Give yourself the freedom to admit that you don't have all the answers, that this is harder than you expected, that it's not always fun. You don't have to be the poster family for adoption.

In 2002 more than 66,000 children were adopted domestically and 20,099 children were adopted internationally. Although there are stresses whenever family dynamics change, the vast majority of these adoptions are highly successful. Depending on which report you read, estimates are that somewhere between ten and twenty percent of adoptions disrupt. The majority of these are older children and children with special needs. That seems rather high, but it also means that between eighty and ninety percent of adoptions are successful placements. Of course there are highly publicized cases where children and young people who were adopted develop major problems in life, but remember that plenty of people who weren't adopted face these same problems.

There will certainly be interesting moments as you and your child adjust to each other. Prepare for the unexpected. Be ready to laugh and remember that many behaviors aren't wrong, they're just different than what you're accustomed to. A year from now you'll quite likely look back at these early days with amusement and amazement at how far you've all come.

Adoption is about permanent, loving families *for children*. With all their bad habits, various disorders, delays, and discipline issues, children are priceless creations of their heavenly Father, knit together in their mothers' wombs, bought with a price. We are reminded that blessed is the man whose quiver is full of them.

Enjoy the journey as you and your child become a family!

"I know the plans I have for you," declares the Lord. "Plans for good and not for evil, to give you a future and a hope." Jeremiah 29:11

Introduction

Throughout this book I refer to stories involving my own children to illustrate the situations I'm asking you to consider. I am very aware that our family is fallible and that we are not unique in our experiences. The children have agreed to be vulnerable in the hope that their stories might be of benefit to other families. Please understand that we are not claiming to have always made the right decisions with our children. I simply share with you choices we have made and ways we have handled challenges in order to get you thinking of what will work best for your family.

The children have given us permission to share these parts of their lives with you and we pray as a family that our experiences will help other families adjust, bond and point still more families to the joy of learning to glorify God in more and more aspects of their lives.

In order for you to understand these stories, I'll introduce you briefly to the members of The Gardner Gang!

Peter, our oldest son, was born to Steve and me in 1984. He is a tall, gentle young man who attends Multnomah Bible College and anticipates spending his life in overseas missions. He has been instrumental in our adoption journey, eagerly welcoming each new child. John and Andrew adore Peter, hanging on him whenever he is home. Peter always makes time for the younger children. We can tell he will be a wonderful father someday!

Aaron, our second son, was born to Steve and me in 1986. He attends Eastern Washington University and is majoring in journalism, and is looking forward to graduating and having a family and career. He has not been as excited about our adoptions as the other children have, partially because he doesn't especially enjoy young children. Nevertheless, he has done a great job of pitching in and helping around the house to make our large family function.

Susannah, our birth daughter, was born in 1988. She thoroughly enjoys being an older sister and is generally kind and helpful with the younger ones. As a result of seeing the needs of her adopted siblings, she plans to become an occupational therapist and work in an orphanage overseas. She traveled with me to Ethiopia to bring home Andrew and Dinah three months ago. It was a very eye-opening experience for her and she says her career plans were definitely confirmed.

Rebekah was born in 1989 and arrived at the orphanage within a week of her birth. We adopted her from Jiangsu province, China in 1995, when she was five years old. She was born with a cleft lip and palate and received very little attention in her orphanage. At the time of her adoption her speech and language skills were extremely delayed, about the level of a two year old. Now in middle school, she has made wonderful progress but continues to struggle with issues of speech and language.

Deborah, our second adopted child, was born in Smolensk, Russia in 1992. Born three months prematurely and without arms, her birthmother chose not to take her home from the hospital. She spent the first year of her life in a Russian hospital and then was moved to an orphanage. Four years old at the time we adopted her in 1997, she was very verbal and extremely strong-willed. Instead of arms she has short stubs, each with a single digit. She is highly capable and can accomplish most tasks by using a combination of her feet and stubs.

John was born in 1991 and joined our family in 2001. He is from a tribal area in Orissa state, India. Because he developed an eye infection when he was very young, one of his eyeballs was removed and he has less than 20/700 vision in the other eye. He spent the first six years of his life with his birthmother and lived in his orphanage for three years. Arriving in our family as an extremely introverted child, he has blossomed. He reads Braille, competes in track events with sighted children, and plays the trumpet in the school band.

Andrew, born in 1995, joined our family three months ago in May of 2004. He is from the Wolayta region of Ethiopia. After the death of his parents he cared for his little sister alone for several months until a missionary doctor brought them to an orphanage in Addis Ababa. In February, with our adoption paperwork nearly ready to go to the Ethiopian court, we

15

learned that Andrew's precious little sister Tsahaynesh had died. Three months later he was in our home, with much to grieve and many adjustments to make. He is fitting in well, though sometimes finds it difficult to admit that he needs parents after having managed reasonably well on his own.

Dinah was born in August of 2003 and also joined our family in May of 2004. When Tsahaynesh died Andrew indicated he would still like a little sister. Dinah had arrived at the orphanage as a tiny premature baby, not expected to live. At the time of Tsahaynesh' death Dinah's survival was no longer in question, but her motor skills were extremely delayed. Other families had turned down her referral, but we felt her alertness and responsiveness were positive signs and decided to welcome her into our family. In her first two months home she has blossomed into a very smiley, content little one.

So that's the family! They've each provided us with joys and challenges, and we can't imagine life without any of them. We are eagerly watching to see the Lord's plan unfold in each of their lives.

The Gardner kids in 2004

PART ONE

Looking At Our Hearts

CHAPTER ONE

Emotions That Might Surprise You

~~~

After having worked so hard to adopt you might be surprised at some of the emotions you feel.

LET DOWN

It's common after working hard for a major event in life to feel let down when it's over. Because you've put so much effort into accomplishing your adoption you may feel a bit blue now and wonder why when you finally have your longed for child in your home.

Years ago I delightedly planned my wedding. After a wonderful day of celebration and fun I couldn't understand why I felt so weepy in the evening. Since then I've learned this is not at all an uncommon reaction to the fulfillment of a dream.

One of my favorite Shel Silverstein poems in his book *Where the Sidewalk Ends* is "The Search":

THE SEARCH

I searched to find the pot of gold
That's waiting where the rainbow ends
I searched and searched and searched and searched
And searched and searched, and then—
There it was, deep in the grass,
Under an old and twisty bough.
It's mine! It's mine! It's mine at last!
What do I search for now? (1)

Don't be surprised if you feel kind of blue for awhile after adopting. It sometimes takes awhile to develop a new focus after working on one thing for so long.

GRIEF

It might seem surprising to think you would grieve about an adoption. After all, isn't this what you've been pursuing wholeheartedly? Yet much as you love your child you may struggle with the realization that this isn't the child to whom you might have given birth. You may grieve the loss of a child who looks like you, has your mannerisms, and shares your genes. It can take awhile to learn that the surprises inherent in raising an adopted child are a wonderful part of the adventure.

It's also possible to grieve for the child you might have adopted had you not adopted the child you did. This may sound a bit confusing, but it's a natural feeling nevertheless. Sometimes you look at the children your friends adopted and find your child lacking by comparison. You might wish you'd adopted a child of a different age or gender. Occasionally you might learn of a waiting child and wish you could add him or her to your family, but you can't because you have to finalize your new child's adoption first.

When things aren't going as you would have liked Proverbs 3:5,6 is helpful. "Trust in the Lord with all your heart and lean not on your own understanding. In all your ways acknowledge Him and He will make your paths straight." The Lord isn't capricious in His dealings with us. If you approached your adoption with an attitude of seeking the Lord's direction and asked Him to open and close doors in your pursuit of a child, you can trust that the child in your home is the right child for your family. Even if you ran headlong into adopting a particular child and didn't seek the Lord's direction, this is the child the Lord is allowing you to raise. This is your child in every sense of the word. It may take time to feel a connection with this child, but it helps if you begin to try to study your child and learn as much as you can about this little person. Avoid comparisons and begin to relate to this child for the unique individual she is.

TIREDNESS

You're tired. You're tired of being tired. And it's frustrating when you know that everyone expects you to be perky and thrilled with your new child. After all, it's all you've talked about for the last several months. You've asked for prayer about bringing your child home quickly. Now she's here, and everyone thinks you should be the happiest parent on the planet. And maybe you are. But maybe, deep down, you wonder if life will ever again be as good as it was before. Safe. Comfortable. Predictable. Maybe those parts of your life that seemed so dull look awfully appealing now.

And the hard thing is there's no one to talk to about your feelings! If you mention your tiredness people are likely to shrug it off, thinking, "You have what you wanted. Now live with it!" There is very little awareness that your whole family is going through a huge period of adjustment.

Perhaps your spouse doesn't even understand. If you longed to adopt a child more than your spouse did, he or she may be a bit unsympathetic to your feelings now. Your spouse may feel that he let you pursue your dream, and now it's time to get on with life. Or she might even say those dreaded words, "I told you so!"

Sibling Emotions

On top of your own issues in dealing with your new child, you might have other children who are having their own adjusting to do. In many families children are firmly behind their parents' adoption plans. In other cases they have reluctantly supported the idea, or been downright resistant. Now the new child is home, and your other children have a tremendous amount of adjusting to do. Even if they longed for the arrival of their new sibling, they probably had no idea of the extent of the changes that would happen in their lives.

It's easy to be so wrapped up in the needs of the new child that we put the needs of our other children on hold. They miss the time we were able to spend just with them. They get annoyed when their new brother gets into their things. They might even resent all the attention everyone gives the new child.

When we added Andrew and Dinah to our family recently, our eleven year old daughter, who had been the youngest child for seven years, struggled for several weeks. Not only had she been the baby of the family, but due to her physical limitations (she was born without arms) she hadn't been expected to do all of the chores we required of the older children. It was a wake up call to all of us when we realized that we had neglected to help her learn the skills we had required of our other children at her age. So not only did she have to adjust to not quite getting as much attention as before, but she also had to grow up in many ways. Obviously this was rather stressful for her.

When a new baby joins a family the older children need to learn to share their parents' time and attention. But when an older child joins the family it affects the amount of time and money the family has available for each child perhaps even more. The older children will be asked to help out in various ways. If the new sibling is bossy, noisy or otherwise obnoxious it can be difficult for everyone. Parents need to be sure they are not devoting so much attention to the new arrival that the other children feel neglected.

It helps if you can assist your children in feeling that they play a very important role in helping the new child adjust to the family. You can explain that the new child will learn your family's routines and habits by watching the other children. Spend time with your children, make sure they feel a part of the whole adoption adventure, let them know how proud of them you are, and allow them to share their frustrations with you. Sometimes just knowing that you're sometimes frustrated, too, can help with the adjustment.

So what can you do? How can you get past these early days of adjusting and wondering in your heart of hearts if you really did make a mistake?

Talk with people who've been there. Nearly every adoptive family goes through some degree of adjustment fatigue and grief. Don't hesitate to be open and share your feelings. Quite likely you'll soon realize you are far from alone. And seeing how other families have adjusted and how well life is going can give you hope that you'll soon be over this hard time, too.

Take care of yourself. The stresses you are facing are every bit as real as those faced by families who have just given birth. You need to sleep when your baby sleeps or declare an hour rest time for everyone after lunch. Cut back on outside activities, even at church, and concentrate on building your family. Eat well, even if that means enlisting someone else to cook for awhile. Be sure to exercise. Family walks are healthy for everyone. And be sure to reserve time just for your spouse. You need to share your feelings and see what you can do to support each other. As much as you are committed to your new child, remember that eventually he or she will leave your home, and your relationship with your spouse will continue. Keep that relationship strong.

So how long are we talking about? Will life be back to normal within a month? Don't count on it! It normally takes at least six months to assimilate a new child into your family. Often it might take a year. At the end of that time you will probably be able to look back and see tremendous growth in your family. The Lord may have reasons for this adoption that you weren't even considering. He can use this not just to provide a family for your child, but to humble you and your whole family before Him.

Finally, if things get really overwhelming, it is appropriate to seek counseling. You certainly won't be the first person to struggle through this adjustment period. Don't let things get out of control.

Notes

1. Shel Silverstein, *Where the Sidewalk Ends* (New York: Harper and Row, 1974), 166.

CHAPTER TWO

Why You Got Involved with Adoption

⟶⟵

When you get discouraged parenting your adopted child, it helps to remember why you made the decision to adopt in the first place. There are as many reasons as there are adoptive families. Some people desperately long for a child. Others see a need and want to help meet it. Still others have enjoyed parenting and want to continue to do so. Unless you were motivated by sin, such as pride or the desire to draw attention to yourself, one reason is not necessarily better than another.

Consider this: when you decided to adopt, was it for you, or was it for a child? We do a lot of things ostensibly to meet someone else's needs, but deep down we're trying to meet needs of our own. If you adopted because of problems in your marriage, severe loneliness in your life, or a desire to have people notice you, your adoption is not doomed to failure. But it will help if you admit your motivation to yourself and recognize that this child isn't going to solve bigger problems.

Scripture is full of evidence that God has a special heart for the fatherless. Throughout the Old Testament the Israelites are enjoined to help the fatherless and defend their cause. In Psalm 68:5 we're told: "A father of the fatherless and a judge for the widows is God in His holy habitation."

JAMES 1:27

Are we foolhardy to reach out to a child to whom we have no obligation and bring him into our home? Or are we wrong when we say that we have no obligation? What of James 1:27—"Religion that God our Father accepts as pure and faultless is this: to look after orphans and widows in their distress and to keep oneself from being polluted by the world."

There are clearly two aspects to the religion that God accepts—one is an outward display of love and the other an inward development of holiness. Both are critical. It isn't enough simply to be a moral person, but there must be an outward expression of that inward morality manifested in caring for those who can't care for themselves.

The Greek word "orphanos" is rendered "fatherless" in several translations. In John 14:18 the same word is translated "comfortless" or "orphans" when Jesus says He will not leave the disciples permanently (comfortless or as orphans) but will return to them. Ultimately He will send the Holy Spirit to remain with them as a comforter forever.

Apparently James wasn't only speaking of an orphan in the strict sense of having neither father nor mother, but a child who doesn't have anyone to permanently care for him.

Taken this way, an orphan can be any child who doesn't have a permanent family, for any reason. This would include children in foster care and institutions as well as children who are literal orphans.

James tells us to look after orphans in their distress, or as some translations read, to "visit" them in their distress. The Greek word "episkeptomai" does not merely mean to go to see, but to relieve the problems. It is also used in Matthew 25:36 and 43 in reference to caring for the needs of someone sick or in prison. Not a shallow term, it implies a commitment to fully meet the needs of the person to whom we minister. James indicates that this type of commitment results from an outpouring of a heart determined to follow the Lord rather than follow the world's standards.

SOCIETY'S VIEW OF CHILDREN

Life can be so much more than what we Americans have settled for. We have come to believe that comfort and security are our rights. In fact, a large portion of society considers children not worth the time, effort and expense involved in raising them. A recent front-page article in the Spokane Spokesman-Review mentioned a couple approaching forty who had never had children. The wife said they never thought they had quite enough money for a family. "Kids seem to be a luxury item nowadays," she stated. (1) Her comments raised my eyebrows. A luxury item—not someone with whom to bake cookies and throw a baseball?

If you have birth children and decide to adopt, or if you adopt more than two children, people are going to think you're odd. They can understand the desire to have a child or two, but more than that and you've gone overboard. It can be stressful to feel as though your family is constantly on display.

If we understand how people view our families and perhaps how, in our heart of hearts, we view them as well, it can help us to evaluate our reasons for adopting.

DINKs and SILKs

Many couples for whom the monetary expense of childrearing isn't an issue feel that kids would take up too much of their time and emotional energy. These people are DINKs—double income, no kids. Compare that to some of our families that we might call SILKs—single income, lots of kids! Some of our friends intentionally decided to remain childless so that they and their wives could pursue careers and hobbies. Now approaching 50, we hear regret in their voices as they wonder who will make decisions for them when they are older and who will visit them when they've retired. They realize that the children they might have had would be in their twenties by now, long past the messy, time-consuming stage, and could have been their best friends. Now they hope that their friends' children will provide companionship and decision making as the years go by.

Idol Children

Another large portion of society sees children not as a nuisance but almost as their idols. Many couples choose to have one or two perfect children, preferably a boy and a girl, and to let their lives completely revolve around those children throughout their childhood. The children's activities and wishes run the household. My husband is a pastor to children and families. Sometimes we have commented to a couple that we missed seeing them in church for a few weeks, only to have them reply, "Oh, Tyler didn't want to come so we stayed home." Eight year old Tyler had the right—and the responsibility—to make decisions for the whole family. Where the family goes, what they eat, how they spend their free time is often decided by these children who become the family's idols. Rather than making decisions based on what will honor the Lord, families make decisions with their children's comfort in mind.

JUST THERE

Another significant segment of society sees children neither as a burden nor as an idol, but simply as part of the background of life. Like food, shelter and clothing they take having kids for granted. Unfortunately a large percentage of this group is, for various reasons, unprepared to parent. Because of their own issues, including poverty, drugs, alcohol and stress, their children often are severely neglected and abused. In the saddest cases the children end up being removed from their homes.

Burdens, idols, something to be taken for granted—that's a pretty sorry description of what a child should be! Let's contrast that with what Scripture says about the value of children.

SCRIPTURE'S VIEW OF CHILDREN

Significantly, the Bible plainly says in Psalm 127 that children are a gift from the Lord. Comparing children to arrows in the hands of a warrior, we are told, "How blessed is the man whose quiver is full of them!" The point is not, as we are often asked, "How big is your quiver?" Rather the blessed man is the one whose life is full of children to train, to raise, to talk with long into late night hours, to delight in seeing growth and maturity take place.

Psalm 139 tells us that the Lord designed each person according to His plan. Each child is of immense worth. "For Thou didst form my inward parts. Thou didst weave me in my mother's womb. I will give thanks to Thee, for I am fearfully and wonderfully made." Every child, regardless of physical or mental capacity, was personally designed by the Lord. Every child deserves a family to love and cherish him. But if you choose to adopt a child with physical, mental or emotional challenges many people will consider you either saintly or stupid. It's difficult for many people to see the value in each child and to understand your obedient response to the Lord's calling.

Jesus demonstrated the value of children when He held them, hugged them and blessed them (Luke 12:2). He went on to say that it would be better for a person to have a millstone—a heavy stone used to grind flour—hung around his neck than to cause a child to stumble That's a pretty big responsibility, and shows how seriously we should take our relationships with children.

Indeed, we are shown in Scripture that there is a great responsibility involved in raising children. As we go through each day we are to spend time with our children and guide them in forming their values.

So the contrast between society's view of children and Scripture's view of children is significant. Rather than being a burden, an idol or something to take for granted Scripture portrays children as a gift, a joy, a privilege and a responsibility.

Too Costly

A common objection to adoption is that it is too expensive and we shouldn't spend so much money on one child. A typical international adoption or healthy domestic infant adoption can range from $10,000 to $30,000. That's indeed an incredible amount of money. The total adoption expenses for our five adopted children have been close to $64,000. We adopted two of the children when we were missionaries in Taiwan and three on a pastor's salary in the States. There are two ways this was possible for us. First, we intentionally chose to cut back our lifestyle to free up money for adoption. Everyone has some discretionary money that can be used for clothes, travel, dinners out, a boat, a new car—we all are going to spend our money on something. To choose to use those resources to give a child a chance to be raised in a Christian family is storing up treasures in heaven.

Second, each time we adopted friends generously helped with the expenses. One couple, who doesn't make a lot more than we do, has given us $1000 toward each adoption. In Taiwan our church took an offering to help. For our most recent adoption someone anonymously donated $10,000, and someone we had never met sold his van and gave us the proceeds. We love seeing people get involved who won't consider adopting personally. Helping financially is a very significant way to make a child's adoption possible and make a difference for eternity. We all spend our resources on something.

During difficult financial times, when investments lose rather than gain funds for their owners, it's encouraging to know that, by investing in children's lives through adoption, we can take our investments into eternity with us.

Too Time-Consuming

Another objection when we talk about adoption is the idea that these children are going to cause us a lot of work. People have asked us why in the world we would want to spend our time caring for children who really aren't our responsibility. Aside from the fun of having a home full of laughter and activity and the significant joy we receive from seeing the children's progress, there is an eternal factor involved as well. Nate Saint, one of the five missionaries martyred by the Auca Indians in the '50s, said, "People ask why in the world we waste our lives as missionaries. They forget that they too are expending their lives . . . and when the bubble has burst they will have nothing of eternal significance to show for the years they have wasted." (2)

John Piper, in his challenging book *Don't Waste Your Life*, says, "Risk is right. And the reason is not because God promises success to all our ventures in his cause. There is no promise that every effort for the cause of God will succeed, at least not in the short run. John the Baptist risked calling King Herod an adulterer when he divorced his own wife in order to take his brother's wife. For this John got his head chopped off. And he had done right to risk his life for the cause of God and truth. Jesus had no criticism for him, only the highest praise (Matthew 11:11)." (3)

He goes on to say, "And now what about you? Are you caught in the enchantment of security, paralyzed from taking any risks for the cause of God? Or have you been freed by the power of the Holy Spirit from the mirage of Egyptian safety and comfort? Do you men ever say with Joab, 'For the sake of the name, I'll try it! And may the LORD do what seems good to him'? Do you women ever say with Esther, 'For the sake of Christ, I'll try it! And if I perish, I perish'?" (4)

So risk is right, if undertaken for the right reasons. Not for self-exaltation, nor to become fixated on self-denial, nor to try to win favor with God. Piper adds, "Every loss we risk in order to make much of Christ, God promises to restore a thousandfold with his all-satisfying fellowship." (5)

Fifty years from now most of us will be dead. A hundred years from now, other than our names on a family tree, no one will even remember that we lived. So what's the point? Should we try to get everything we can out of this life, and pursue all the pleasure available? Or is it wise to see this life as a prelude to eternity? The seventy or eighty years allotted to us now are an eye blink compared to what we have in store for us in eternity. Bringing children who desperately need to know the love of God into our homes, even when it ends up requiring a lot of work, is a sacrifice with which the Lord is

pleased. When we arrive in our eternal home we can anticipate hearing His loving voice telling us, "Come, you who are
blessed of my Father, inherit the kingdom prepared for you
from the foundation of the world. For I was hungry, and you
gave me something to eat; I was thirsty, and you gave Me drink;
I was a stranger, and you invited me in; naked, and you clothed
Me; I was sick, and you visited Me; I was in prison, and you
came to me . . . . Truly I say to you, to the extent that you did
it to one of these brothers of Mine, even the least of them, you
did it to Me" (Matthew 25:34–36, 40).

Notes

1. Spokane Spokesman Review newspaper, August 17, 2003, p.1,2.
2. Nate Saint, www.worldmissions.com/revival_quote.
3. John Piper, *Don't Waste Your Life* (Wheaton, Ill: Crossway Books, 2003), 89.
4. Ibid., 89,90.
5. Ibid., 91.

CHAPTER THREE

Is God Good?

A couple of weeks ago our bright, effervescent niece was in town working on her internship with an accounting firm. She had dinner with us, and afterwards joined us for our evening walk. With eight children, two dogs, bikes, scooters, wagons and a stroller our family's nightly parade tends to be the most exciting thing going on in our quiet neighborhood, made up mostly of retired couples. Sometimes I think people bring out their lawn chairs and lemonade just in time to watch our foray.

As we walked Deanna told us about a car accident, her fault, a few weeks earlier. "The insurance company gave us a new car," she said enthusiastically, "and because it has airbags our car insurance went down! God is so good!"

"Deanna," I said, "suppose you'd been given an old car. Would God still be good?"

"Well, yes!" she agreed.

"What if your insurance had gone up rather than down? Would God still be good?"

She could see my point. "Yes, He would," she replied.

"And what if you had been paralyzed from the neck down? Would God still be good?"

She was quiet for a minute. "You're right, He would," she replied contemplatively. "He's good no matter what."

As Christians, does God guarantee us blessings if we follow Him obediently? "We want the good life," says Larry Crabb in his excellent book *The Pressure's Off.* "We maintain that the good life of legitimate blessings is a worthy goal and one that may be reached by living a faithful life of obedience to biblical principles. Good family relationships, good community experiences, good ministry that provides meaning and personal fulfillment, good experiences of God—we can arrange for these blessings to come our way. All we have to do is live godly lives, pray hard, and expect great things from our great God." (1)

Dr. Crabb goes on to explain that this type of linear thinking—if I do A, God will automatically do B—creates tremendous pressure for us because we can never fulfill our side of the bargain perfectly. When something goes wrong we blame ourselves. But bad parents sometimes have great kids, and wonderful parents sometimes have kids who do terrible things. (2)

We Christians try hard to follow God's principles and then, whether we verbalize it or not, believe that He owes us certain blessings as a result. If we just pray hard enough, be a good spouse, give our children appropriate boundaries, we will be blessed with a good marriage and great kids.

So now you've adopted a child or two and are doing your best to make it work. Perhaps you've attended seminars and read numerous books and magazines about adoption. You know everything there is to know about attachment issues. So of course your adjustment will go well. And maybe it will. But maybe it won't.

God's plan for the world is to bring glory to Himself. He says, "Bring my sons from afar and my daughters from the end of the earth, everyone who is called by my name, whom I created for my glory" (Isaiah 43:6,7). That would seem sinfully proud coming from anyone else, but God is God and is therefore worthy of all glory. He can and does allow things to happen in our lives not only to make us more like Him, but also to bring glory to Himself.

In your adoption journey, how can God be most glorified? It may be through a path you would never have chosen. What can God do to work in your life, your child's life, and the lives of everyone watching you to bring glory to Himself?

Our good friends Greg and Terri Bade have six adopted children. They adopted their second daughter, Sarah, from Bulgaria when she was nineteen months old. Their private facilitator had no medical training and didn't notice anything unusual about this little one. Terri says Sarah was nothing like the pictures and description they had been given of her.

Panic struck in those first few days as it became very obvious that something BIG was amiss with this child. After a series of tests, their pediatricians said she would never walk, talk or potty train due to brain damage. He said she'd probably spend her days in a hospital bed in the living room to be close to the family. This was not what they had anticipated! Terri says the reality was so different than what they had expected that they were very discouraged. Now Sarah is twelve years old. She has many challenges due to a low I.Q., cerebral palsy, and other issues. However, not only does she walk, talk, and use the bathroom on her own, she also reads, sings and can play games with her siblings. Sarah will probably always need to live close to her parents.

"I am embarrassed to say that we would not have adopted Sarah had we known the extent of her needs. We knew nothing about caring for a child with severe disabilities. But through Sarah the Lord opened our hearts to loving other children with challenges, and all of our children but one have come to us with significant special needs. Sarah's life has resulted in many children finding homes with us and other families because we're not afraid of special needs anymore. God has shown us He can change our hearts to meet His. He has used this little girl to change everyone around her!" says Terri.

You too may be struggling with the challenges your child has brought. "This isn't what I signed up for!" may be your heart's cry.

On the other hand, you may be having the time of your life. I love being an adoptive mom. I thrive on it. I am energized by seeing my children make progress in every area of their lives. But that doesn't mean that every minute is fun.

This morning, for example, while I was trying to work on this book John and Andrew were playing a game. Soon I heard Andrew laughing and John saying, "That's not nice!"

Turns out that since John is almost completely blind he missed a move in the game, and Andrew thought it was funny. "John no can see, so I win!" he said joyfully.

We talked about kindness and empathy, most of which seemed to go right over Andrew's head. Ten minutes later I heard loud squeals from the backyard. "Andrew, knock it off!" cried John.

Looking out, I saw that Andrew was spraying John with water. I intervened, telling them to change into dry clothes, and then talked with Andrew again. "I think you and John need a break from each other," I said, and proceeded to explain why.

When I finished my explanation Andrew said, "What broke?"

"Nothing broke," I said.

"Yes," he said. "You say break!"

With a sigh and a laugh I realized my explanation had been wasted on Andrew due to his limited English. I sent John off to read Braille and gave Andrew two pages of math problems to do. Not a very good solution, but at least they both settled down.

These are normal sibling squabbles, though the fact that the children are adopted might bring extra issues with which to deal, such as limited English and blindness, but for the most part the issues are the same as those presented by any children. A lot of what's required is just parenting skills, and we often learn those as we go along.

So I encourage you to admit to yourself when things are a bit challenging. Recognize that the outcome of raising your child isn't all up to you. Even if you could be a perfect parent your child might make choices of which you wouldn't be proud. There are no guarantees with biological children either. As Dr. Crabb encourages us, we need to want God Himself more than we want His blessings. (3) Trust Him for the outcome of your adoption journey. As you focus on getting to know God rather than on looking good in front of people, you're in for more joy than you might ever have thought possible.

Notes

1. Larry Crabb, *The Pressure's Off* (Colorado Springs, Colorado: Waterbrook Press, 2002), 30.
2. Ibid., 32.
3. Ibid, 34.

PART TWO

Looking At Our Homes

There are hundreds of books available on raising adopted children, and it's easy to convince ourselves that if we just read enough of them and put all the advice into practice, our family life will go smoothly and we'll raise perfect children. But that puts a lot of pressure on us. When we realize that the Lord is in control of our family and that every child and every situation is unique it helps take the pressure off. We may make different choices for our family than our friends make for their families, and all of us can bring glory to the Lord.

The second part of this book contains suggestions and ideas for the issues you need to consider as you raise your adopted child. Please understand that with most issues there are no right answers. I am not suggesting that the choices our family has made are the choices you should make. We've made plenty of mistakes along the way. I share these ideas and anecdotes to give you a starting place for your thinking. I urge you to evaluate these suggestions and carefully decide what is appropriate for your child and your family. Remember that it will probably take your family several months to adjust to a new member. It will be rewarding to look back a year from now and see how far you've all come.

CHAPTER FOUR

Meeting Your Child and Time Away From Home

THE MEETING

Whether you're traveling overseas or across the United States, after dreaming so long about this moment actually meeting your child can be a surreal experience. With so many people watching this initial meeting any hope of normal emotions surfacing is a pretty unreal expectation. Quite likely you won't feel love at first sight. You might actually wonder what you've gotten into. Don't worry if this first meeting doesn't go well. You have a lifetime together ahead of you.

JUST GET HOME!

It's difficult to really establish boundaries and procedures until you're in your own home. When we were in Russia adopting Deborah our host family was very annoyed that we were trying to establish rules and boundaries for her. Because of her physical challenges they felt we were too firm with her.

We knew that we needed to have the same expectations for her behavior that we do for our other children and that we wouldn't be doing her any favors if we felt sorry for her. However, because our host family's feelings were so clear we realized that we needed to respect their feelings while we were in their home. As frustrating as it was to have to ignore our new daughter's unacceptable behavior we knew we would be home in our own environment in several days and could begin shaping behavior at that point. When things are frustrating on your adoption trip just keep telling yourself that things will get better when you're home. Take one day at a time and get through it. Soon those initial days will be a memory to laugh over.

SPIRITUAL VALUES

Begin from the first day to pray with and for your child. Let your child see how important prayer is to you. Pray at meals and bedtime for sure. You want your child to learn that this is your family's habit even before he or she can understand your words. Children in some countries have religious backgrounds and are familiar with prayer. When we adopted Andrew from Ethiopia we knew he was from an Orthodox background. He clearly understood that we were praying. We asked him to participate but he hesitated because of his limited English. When we assured him that he could pray in Amharic he enjoyed participating in prayer time. For some of our children prayer was unfamiliar. For many days we matter of factly explained to the children that we were talking to God. It was never long until the children wanted to join in. We well remember Rebekah's first five year old prayer: "God, Mommy, Daddy, food, good, one, two, three, I love you!"

While in your child's country you might want to visit a local church. Nearly every large city has an International Church, commonly interdenominational in theology and style and attended by English-speaking expatriates as well as local residents. Attending this type of church is an interesting experience, but it is rather similar to many American churches. If you want a cultural experience more unique to your child's country you might want to consider attending a local church. Your facilitator or guide should be able to tell you about something appropriate.

We had connections with several believers in China, but were asked not to contact them or attend their underground church. They were in a rather precarious position with the government at the time and didn't want us to draw attention to them. There are official state churches in China and it would have been possible to attend one of those.

In Russia in 1997 many churches were just being turned back over to the congregations after having been used for other purposes for many years under communism. We visited several churches and always found a very somber crowd. In fact, our hostess commented that the people were staring at me because I was smiling, and she urged me to look more somber myself! If I had it to do over again I would make an effort to locate and visit an evangelical church. I think we would have had a very different experience, and it would have been fascinating to talk with Russian believers.

Because we knew that Andrew was from an Orthodox background, we asked our guide, who was also orthodox, to take us to a church service with him. He told Susannah and me that we needed to cover our heads with shawls, and took us to a store to purchase them. The bright colors were lovely. Susannah selected a beautiful peach colored shawl and I chose a bright purple one.

The next day when our driver arrived we were ready to go, with our beautiful shawls covering our heads. He said we were appropriately dressed. However, as we drove toward the church we noticed hundreds of people walking toward the building. Everyone was wearing a white cotton gauze shawl. There wasn't a bright color in the crowd. Selamneh's eyes grew big as he laughed and said he had forgotten that it was a special holiday. Oh well, he said, this way he would be able to keep track of us!

Selamneh, my brother-in-law David, and Andrew went over to the men's side of the courtyard. Susannah, Dinah and I went to the women's side. Due to the special holiday there were thousands of people pushing in from every side. Everyone stood for the entire service. Of course we couldn't understand a word that was said, but we enjoyed hearing the congregation join in the chanting occasionally. We managed quite well for the first hour. Then Dinah got fussy. I whipped out a bottle and fed her, quite proud of myself for managing so well in my tiny squished in area. That kept her happy for a little while, and then she got tired of being held.

Ethiopian women eagerly reached out their hands for her, offering her their keys or jewelry with which to play. Dinah was passed from woman to woman, but after a short time she turned and reached her arms out to me. It was tremendously touching to see that after just a few days with me she already felt that was where she belonged.

After awhile Susannah and I began to feel that we had caused enough commotion for the women in our area. We picked up the diaper bag and pushed our way through the crowd to a place where we saw some other friendly faces. We were just beginning to disrupt their worship with our noisy baby when we saw Dave, Selamneh and Andrew approach us with frightened looks on their faces. "We thought we'd lost you in this crowd of people!" they whispered. "Good thing you had on your bright shawls!"

Hastily we all worked our way through the crowd and out the courtyard. We had lasted about two hours, and Selamneh told us that the service would continue for at least five more hours. We were very glad we'd gone, but two hours were enough for us!

BE THE PARENT

When we first meet our new children it can be overwhelming for all of us. Here's a child whose habits, temperament, history and language we scarcely know. The temptation can be to try to win the child's affections by being overly kind and sympathetic. However, in order to prevent problems later at home, it's important to establish yourself as the parent from the start. You may have a facilitator or host family with whom your child seems more comfortable than you. These people can be of invaluable assistance with translation and explanations. However, it is helpful to your child in the long run if it is clear that you are in charge and the facilitator is helping your child with your permission.

You have the right to make decisions such as what time your child will go to bed and what you will offer your child to eat. You didn't adopt this child so you can be her best friend, you adopted her to be her parent.

WHILE YOU WAIT

Often in international adoption families must spend several days in the child's country while waiting for paperwork to be completed. This time can be incredibly frustrating or extremely special. It's a good idea to ask your adoption agency for names of other families who adopted children of a similar age to yours. You can contact these families and ask what they enjoyed doing during the time in country.

You'll want to avoid making your days too busy. Your child will be dealing with many adjustments in food, clothing and relationships. A bit of down time each day will give you an opportunity to begin to get to know each other.

Depending on the age and temperament of your child, visiting local sites can be very enjoyable. Of course you will want to take lots of pictures and video footage. Although your child may not remember much of your time in his country, he will greatly treasure these visual reminders.

If there is a zoo or a place to go swimming your child will quite likely enjoy these activities. Sightseeing may be a very pleasurable activity for you, but might not be a lot of fun for your child. Be sure you don't make the days too long.

When we were in China adopting Rebekah, Steve had to leave after several days in order to complete his teaching assignment for the year. On my own with a five year old, I wasn't inclined to do much sightseeing. Each day we went for walks around the hotel and we spent quite a bit of time swimming in the pool at the White Swan Hotel. It wasn't necessary to fill each day with activity. We both enjoyed the slow pace and the time to get acquainted.

You may like to visit a site of historical or cultural interest in which your child has very little interest. When in India we had several extra days and decided to visit the Taj Mahal and Gandhi's cremation site. They were very fascinating experiences for Steve and me. Nine year old John wasn't particularly interested in seeing these things, so we tried to make the days fun for him by stopping for ice cream and other treats that he enjoyed. Three years later, however, he very much enjoys looking at the pictures of himself at these places and is glad we visited these important sites.

If possible, try to see more than just a large city. Many children are from rural areas, and it is a wonderful experience to hire a driver to take you out of town to more remote locations. You'll see different housing and clothing styles and get a better feel for the country you are visiting.

TIME AT THE ORPHANAGE

Depending on the country from which you are adopting, opportunities to spend time in your child's orphanage or foster care situation will vary. In some countries a cursory visit is allowed. When we were adopting from India and Ethiopia we were allowed to spend as much time as we liked, over several days, in our sons' orphanages. These were wonderful, insightful days. We were able to meet the boys' teachers and housemothers as well as the orphanage directors. The most enjoyable time at the orphanages, however, was getting to know the other children.

In both countries we were swarmed by our sons' friends and classmates. Especially in Ethiopia older boys sidled up to me and begged, "Take my picture! Find me a family!" We took dozens of pictures and spent time with the boys so we could describe them to interested families. Besides helping these boys our son enjoys wistfully looking at the pictures and remembering his friends.

When we planned our trip to Ethiopia we wanted to do something for Andrew's friends and the other children in the orphanage. We knew that some of them may never be adopted and we wanted them to have a special memory. We received permission from the director of the orphanage to plan a party for one hundred of the children, ranging from two or three years old to about fourteen.

My fifteen year old daughter, Susannah, traveled to Ethiopia with me. We had a great deal of fun in the weeks before our trip, planning for this party. We scoured garage sales and close out deals and purchased party hats, tablecloths, noisemakers, balloons, streamers, Easter eggs which we filled with candy, and a small present for each child. We prepared gift bags for each of the children with stickers, pencils, and little kaleidoscopes.

The morning of the party we purchased pastries. Then we arrived at the orphanage and decorated the party room. The children obviously had been told something special was happening, and they tried to peer into the room as we worked. Everyone's anticipation was building.

When everything was ready the children lined up outside and filed into the party room. Handing each child a gift bag and a party hat, we tried to give Bob the Builder hats to the boys and jeweled hats to the girls. It didn't always work, but the children didn't seem to care. I'll never forget a very simple nine year old boy, who had spent much of his life in a hospital. As I handed him his hat he took my hands, kissed me on both cheeks, and fervently said, "Thank you! Thank you!"

Of course not everything went according to our plans. We planned a game in which each child had a balloon tied to his or her ankle. We divided the children into age groups and they were to try to step on other children's balloons and break them while protecting their own balloons. The younger age groups enjoyed this game thoroughly and everyone else sat in a circle around them and watched. The nine year olds, however, took the game so seriously that I thought they'd end up bloody and sore before they would let anyone stamp on their balloon! We had to end the game with three nine year old winners and not let the older children play.

When planning presents for the children I had selected Hot Wheels cars for the younger boys and Super Balls for the older ones. We had brought Kelly dolls (Barbie's little sister) for the younger girls and cute coin purses for the older ones. A bit of a riot ensued as the children realized they were each going to get a gift. Enlisting the help of some of the older ones, we lined the children up, youngest first, and they came for their gifts. When the ten and eleven year old girls came the plan was for them to select a coin purse. Quickly it became apparent that most of them really wanted a doll instead. Wishing we had brought more, we allowed the girls to take the beautiful little princess dolls. It was heartrending to see thirteen year old girls obviously treasuring their first doll.

Andrew, our son, thoroughly enjoyed this party. He helped stuff the gift bags the night before and played the role of congenial host to the hilt. Because he was from a rural area and didn't speak the national language like most of the other children did, his status in the orphanage had been rather low. This party was a nice way for him to graciously give a treat to his friends.

SHOPPING

You will certainly want to do some shopping while in your child's country. Your child will enjoy having some familiar things in his new home. The most fun part about shopping overseas is that in most of the countries from which people adopt prices are very low. Some suggestions you might want to consider are:

- a nativity scene. *We have one from each of our children's birth countries except India. These are a wonderful way of visualizing for the children that Christ came for the whole world, and that Christianity is not primarily a western religion.*
- national clothing. *Although your children will outgrow it, national clothing is a fun item to have. You can*

have the children's pictures taken in these clothes so they can remember them long after they are outgrown.

- children's tapes. *Children typically enjoy music from their country. You might try to find tapes or CDs of national children's songs.*

- national décor. *With children from several different countries, we have cultural items from around the world decorating our home. From China we have an abacus, wall hangings, a tea set, and name chops. From Russia we have matryoshka dolls, a samavar, and a beautiful painting. From India we have pillows, a beautiful rug, a small table, and a whole row of elephants. From Ethiopia we have a large injera basket, a coffee set, and Ethiopian crosses. Our home is very eclectic in its style and the children very much enjoy having these familiar items around.*

- musical instruments. *If your family enjoys music, it can be fascinating to purchase instruments from your child's country. Drums, guitars, wooden flutes, and other instruments are readily available.*

- food. *It's a good idea to purchase some local snacks to enjoy in the early weeks at home. If you find a local store with a worker who speaks English, you can tell her that you are adopting a child from the area and want your child to have snacks to remember her country. I've always found workers quite willing to show me what snacks and spices I should purchase.*

- tablecloths. *I started a tablecloth collection for my mother as we traveled to various countries. Tablecloths are easy to find in each country and they are a practical gift to give.*

I heard of a woman who purchased enough items on her adoption trips to be able to give each child a gift from his or her country each year on their adoption day until they turned eighteen. What a fun idea for the children, and what a great excuse to shop!

MEETING AT THE AIRPORT

Give some thought to what sort of welcoming committee will greet you on your arrival home. Consider the age and background of your child and the length of your trip as you decide who to invite. Your child has just gone through the very overwhelming experience of meeting new parents. A huge welcoming committee, while fun and affirming for you, may be too much for your child. For other children it may be very exciting. Don't hesitate to change plans after meeting your child if you determine what you had already planned might be too much for this child.

WELCOME PARTY

The same consideration should be given to a welcoming party for your child. It's natural to want everyone to share in your joy and meet your child. Quite likely many of your friends have been praying for you and are eager to see the fruition of all your dreams. Be cautious about too many gifts and too much excitement, however. For a child from overseas or foster care a lot of attention and new possessions might be overwhelming rather than fun.

CHAPTER FIVE

First Days At Home

The first days and weeks at home can be overwhelming to your new child. Whether from overseas or foster care, your child may feel like he has arrived on a different planet! Everything seems unfamiliar. Try to remember a situation you may have been in sometime when you weren't sure how you were supposed to act. Visiting your child's country may be an example. Imagine not having anyone to talk with about your feelings and thinking that everyone else around you knows exactly how to fit it. Your child can feel very vulnerable. Understanding common feelings that children experience may help you to know how to make things less overwhelming for your child.

BEDROOM

You've spent weeks creating a beautiful pink bedroom with a canopy bed for your soon-to-be-home daughter. It seems like every little girl's dream room, and you hope she'll spend hours enjoying it. American society tells us that children value their own bedroom. Yet for many children the very idea of being alone in a room at night is a frightening thought. Privacy isn't a possibility, yet alone a value, in an orphanage or many foster homes. Our children, adopted at nine months, four, five, nine and nine and a half years old, didn't like to be alone even during the day, let alone at night. John, adopted from India at age nine, constantly followed us from room to room. He absolutely refused to be by himself at any time. When his older brothers who shared his room were gone overnight John begged to sleep on the couch rather than alone downstairs. After two years he finally felt courageous enough to sleep in a room with only the dog for company.

Many children haven't slept in American-type beds. Pillows, sheets and soft mattresses may be unfamiliar to them. Many families, when they check on them at night, find their children sleeping on the floor. Wise parents will make sure their child feels comfortable and safe at night.

CLOTHES

A closet full of dresses and a bureau full of neatly folded outfits may seem like the perfect welcome-home treat for your new child. So why does your daughter wear the same two outfits over and over again?

Some items of clothing might be unfamiliar to your child. Many children haven't worn shoes, underwear or short pants before. Pajamas are often also a novelty.

New parents often want to shower their child with cute outfits, not realizing that too many choices can be difficult. Three or four outfits may be plenty at first, with additional new clothes added slowly.

Although shoes are a necessity, they may feel tight and constricting to children who have seldom worn them. Sandals, ballet slippers, or shoes a size too large may be a helpful compromise at first.

TOYS

One of the joys of parenthood is getting to play with toys all over again as we share experiences with our children. It can be disappointing when older children arrive home and don't seem interested in playing with Legos, dolls or toy cars.

Many children are from environments where they have had few or no toys available. Private ownership of toys or other possessions isn't allowed in many orphanages. Children who have gone through a series of foster homes typically don't have much to call their own either. When these children join our families it's easy to want to give them everything on which they've missed out. But children can feel overwhelmed by too many things at once.

Additionally, many children really don't understand how to play. It seems strange to think that this is a skill a child wouldn't have, but quite often the children have simply run around outside, playing soccer and other outdoor games, or watched videos. They haven't learned to play creatively.

You might give your child one new toy at a time and spend time with her, showing her how to use it and, in the case of a doll, for example, engaging in pretend play with your child. You might set aside a certain amount of time each day where your child is to play quietly with toys you provide, perhaps with you as playmate. Eventually your child will learn to play on his own and with other children.

"I WANT"

Unfortunately, children can begin to feel that they are entitled to have everything that everyone else in the family has. When I picked up Andrew in Ethiopia I gave him a nice pair of tennis shoes. He liked them very much, and thanked me over and over for them. Upon our arrival home, however, he saw that his brothers not only had tennis shoes, but black shoes to wear to church as well. This bothered him a great deal. Then he realized that John, who is a junior Olympics runner, also had running shoes. He assured me that he liked to run, also, and needed special shoes. I reminded him that just ten days earlier he had been thrilled with his new tennis shoes. Obviously that was then and this was now, however. Church shoes and running shoes became his obsession.

Two months into his American life, Andrew has a very long list of "I wants." Many are reasonable items that he sees his siblings have, but I am not about to go buy him everything they have accumulated over several years. He receives a small allowance and I regularly remind him that he could purchase one of the things he wants with his money. "No!" he tells me. "You my mommy, you buy!" So he must wait.

This sense of entitlement seems quite common among older adopted children. You will need to carefully decide how you will help your child feel like a full-fledged member of the family without feeling you need to buy her everything at once.

INVESTIGATIVE BEHAVIOR

"Don't touch! Careful, that might break! Oh, no!" We use those words while helping a toddler learn what is appropriate to touch, and when we adopt older children it's easy to feel like we have a toddler in the house all over again.

Our American homes are full of interesting items our children have never seen before. There is so much to look at, figure out, and explore! It's a good idea to keep a rather close eye on your child in his early days in your home. Because the children don't understand the purpose of many items they may use them improperly.

A few days after John arrived home I noticed a small piece of wallpaper torn off our kitchen wall. I thought someone had bumped into the wall with something. Later in the day I noticed another piece missing, which seemed odd. I decided to do some chores at the dining room table where I could keep an eye on the kitchen. Half an hour later John ambled into the room. He started scratching the wall until he loosened a piece of wallpaper and pulled it off. He held it up very close to his eye, stared at it for a moment, dropped it on the ground and sauntered off. I called him back, showed him the piece of wallpaper on the floor, and through short words and lots of gestures tried to explain that we want the walls to look pretty and he needed to leave the wallpaper alone. The concept of pretty rather than simply utilitarian was a hard one for him to grasp, and we had to work on it quite a bit.

Another day I went out on the deck in the early morning to have my devotions before everyone else was up. I sat in my wicker furniture—a very long-ago gift from my husband—and prepared to read. But as I picked up my Bible I saw several small piles of wicker around the area. Looking more closely, it was apparent someone had picked little pieces off the furniture in several places.

When the children were up and ready for their day I called them onto the deck and asked who had picked at the furniture. As I expected, everyone except John denied it. He simply refused to answer, and I was pretty sure I'd found the culprit. Again I tried to explain the idea of pretty to him. Then I sent him in the house and talked with the other children, asking them to be on "fidget patrol" and keep an eye on John for awhile.

A week later I purchased a cake with a plastic cover on it from Costco, intending to serve it to some guests for dinner that night. As I worked in the kitchen John stared at the cake from every angle, and then to my surprise he picked the cake up and turned it upside down!

Andrew was also very inquisitive upon his arrival home. One morning he arrived at the breakfast table with shiny, sticky, wet hair. I asked what was on his hair, and initially he claimed nothing. When I pressed him further he took me into the laundry room and showed me the green Spray 'n Wash bottle. He had watched me spray it on clothing, and for some reason only he understood, thought it would clean his hair. I made him take a shower and wash his hair. Since he was already dressed he thought this was extremely unreasonable of me, but I wanted him to learn to ask before trying something, since the next time it might not be quite so harmless.

Later that afternoon I brought in the mail and set it on the dining room table. I left the room for several minutes, and when I returned the mail had been opened and was scattered around! I called together the usual suspects, and Andrew admitted he had opened the mail. He didn't think he had done anything wrong. "You open!" he said, referring to all the times he had watched me open and sort the mail. I spent several minutes helping him understand that some things are mommy's job, not his.

Even though our children are old enough that we think we can safely let them roam the house on their own, it is a good idea to keep a close eye on things in the beginning. There are simply too many new stimuli.

ESTABLISHING ROUTINES

It's summertime, it's been ninety-five degrees for weeks, and I have a bunch of hot, bored kids on my hands.

Each of our older children has arrived without the ability to entertain him or herself. They enjoy playing outside—riding bikes, playing on the swing set, running around the yard—but have no idea what to do inside the house. It's obvious videos and television have been used as babysitters, and the children would be comfortable watching videos by the hour.

It was a shock for Andrew when we were still in Ethiopia and I told him that we don't watch television in our home. "America no have t.v.?" he asked with a gasp. I assured him that there is television in America, but that we don't watch it in our home. I'm sure that for a moment he wondered if joining this family was a big mistake! I told him that we often watch a video as a family on Friday evenings, and that he could help select the video, and he breathed a bit of a sigh of relief.

The children typically don't know how to play with toys, use art materials, or be creative. Steve and I usually spend quite a bit of time with a new child, showing her how to play with Legos, how to paint with watercolors and make things with Play-doh, and how to arrange furniture in a dollhouse. It's important to us that the children don't just run around outside like little street rats, but that they learn to select something to do with their time. It's also important that we have a lot of fun with the kids. We don't want them to see us just as disciplinarians who nag them all the time. We want them to eagerly anticipate the next fun time with mom and dad!

Interestingly, all of our children have arrived home in the late spring. This results in summer, with all its unstructured days, stretching ahead of us. It's always a challenge for me to help a new child fill his time over the first summer. I want to say, "Find something to do!" when I see a child wandering aimlessly around the house, but I remind myself that she really doesn't know how to do so. One of my children's teachers also reminded me that staring into space or wandering aimlessly is not necessarily a bad thing for newly arrived children to do. They have so many new experiences and stimuli to deal with that some down time to process it all can be a very good thing.

Structure and routine go a long way toward making life easier for everyone. If the child knows that at one o'clock every day he will go swimming it gives him something to plan his day around.

Chores are helpful. We find that chores give structure to the day, and the kids are pleased when we compliment them on the good job they've done. Initially it might seem difficult to know what chores to assign to a child who isn't familiar with American homes and cleaning supplies. Sweeping and taking out the trash are jobs that are easy to explain. Kitchen chores are more complex. In his first month with us Andrew broke three glasses by trying to crowd too many things into the dishwasher at once. Although I normally am not bothered by occasional broken dishes, I told Andrew he would need to pay me a quarter if he broke any more glasses. I wanted him to understand that he needed to do the job a bit more carefully. So far, no more broken glasses! You know you've accomplished a degree of routine when you can say to your child "Do your chores, please!" and she knows exactly what is expected.

A week at Vacation Bible School is a fun method of giving structure to a child's summer. Although the child probably won't understand much of what is going on his first year in your home, he will enjoy the games, refreshments and crafts. Story time might seem long if the child has quite limited English.

Doing some schoolwork over the summer is a good idea for several reasons. The children can learn some beginning skills or keep up their skills, they can anticipate working quietly for part of the day, and their English skills receive a boost.

The children will soon learn the routines of your home and enjoy the security of anticipating the same things happening day after day and week after week. If we miss a Friday video and pizza night there had better be a good reason! Our children enjoy saying "We always go to the Bades on the fourth of July" or "Daddy always takes the boys out to breakfast on Saturday mornings."

FOOD ISSUES

"Yum, chicken curry!" John grinned as I brought a steaming hot bowl into the dining room. Then I glanced at Deborah and saw disappointment in her eyes. She doesn't like spicy food.

Food is very significant to most adopted children. Whether from an orphanage or from foster care, many children have never had the opportunity to eat as much as they would like. As a result, many children hoard food, as though they wonder if there really will be another ample meal the next day. It's not unusual to find food stashed away in your child's bedroom.

On our flight from Ethiopia to America rolls were served with dinner. Andrew looked around and noticed that many of the people near him weren't eating their rolls. He asked several people if he could have their rolls, and put them in his backpack. Apparently he was unsure about what he would find in America and wanted to be prepared.

Some children don't seem to know how to tell themselves that they have had enough to eat. Most of our children have sat at the table taking serving after serving and continuing to eat long after everyone else has been excused. We have learned that, at least for awhile, we need to limit the amount the children can eat. We can do this by removing the bowls of food from the table after the child has had two or three servings. We can also set limits to the amount of food the child is allowed to take. For example, when we have pizza nights I tell the children they may have three pieces of pizza. They all enjoy pizza a great deal and would tend to overeat if allowed. By setting a limit they often stretch their slices of pizza out throughout the video and eat at a healthier pace.

A year ago we were on a family vacation, and one of the children complained that she was starving. Another child said, "We don't know what it means to starve!"

Still another commented, "Maybe some of the adopted kids do." And they proceeded to ask the younger children if they had ever had to go for a whole day without eating.

Rebekah and Deborah both commented that they had at least one meal a day in their orphanages. John, however, said that when he lived with his birthmom he had often gone a day without food, and sometimes two or three days.

By now I was intrigued by the conversation, and said to John, "Do you understand what they are asking? Did you ever have to go a whole day with no food at all?"

He assured us that he understood and had indeed gone without food for two or three days.

"John, what did you do? How did you make it through those days?" I asked.

"I drank a lot of water to fill my stomach," he said, "and sometimes I climbed a tree and found a few nuts."

We were all very sober after this conversation, gaining a greater appreciation for all we have and understanding better why John tends to gorge himself at meals.

Children may have had fairly limited food choices and as a result may be hesitant to try unfamiliar foods. Families handle this in different ways. Some families make a good effort to prepare familiar foods for their child for several months. Other families expect the child to adapt more quickly.

With children from five countries in our home it is impossible for me to prepare each child's preferred foods on a regular basis. I don't have time to prepare different food for each child. Over the course of a couple of weeks I prepare a variety of foods, trying to occasionally include the foods I know each child prefers. We tell the children we expect them to eat what is served, and that their favorite foods will be on the menu occasionally. All of our children are good eaters.

For families with fewer children's preferences to consider, preparing ethnic foods more often seems like a wonderful idea if the family chef has time to do so. Families do need to remember, though, that the children will eventually eat in other families' homes or at church events and need to develop familiarity with many types of foods.

ATTITUDES TOWARD AUTHORITY AND WOMEN

"You drive car?" John asked incredulously upon our return home from India.

'Sure, why not?" I asked.

"But you are lady!" he said, shocked that a lowly woman could do something as significant in his eyes as driving a vehicle.

In many countries from which Americans adopt, women's status is still quite low. In India, for example, many girls are available for adoption because families living in poverty don't want to pay a dowry to arrange for yet another daughter to be married. In China, hundreds of thousands of baby girls are abandoned because of the One Child Policy and the strong need families perceive to have a son.

If you adopt an older boy, he may unconsciously have picked up the attitude that males are superior to females. This might affect his attitude not only toward his new mother, but toward his sisters as well.

Beliefs like this that are ingrained in a child can't be changed overnight. Your son needs to see that his sisters, female classmates, and especially his mother have equal status with males. He needs to learn that mother is to be obeyed as much as father. You can explain this idea, but your son will need to observe the treatment of females over a long period of time until he understands that not only are they equal, but to be treated respectfully.

If your son is disrespectful to his new mother it can be helpful if his new father explains that he expects him to talk politely to his mom, and that dad will be listening. Dads can set an example by being polite and respectful to their wives and daughters. Insist on courtesy and obedience.

Single mothers with older sons may run into trouble with this. There should be some men in your son's life who play a significant role. This could be a grandfather, uncle, committed neighbor, or men from church. In any case, there should be one or more men who spend time with your son, modeling masculinity and reinforcing the importance of your son respecting you.

Overreacting to Physical Pain

John rarely shows emotion, absolutely never cries, and seldom is especially happy either. Yet if he falls and scrapes a knee or if he has a headache he becomes extremely upset and sobs. It's as though he has learned to keep his feelings inside, but feels it's safe to show emotion about pain.

I comfort him and show him that I'm trying to alleviate his pain. This is an area in which I want him to learn that he can trust me. I want him to feel comfortable sharing his other emotions with me, so I try to show appropriate sympathy to pain. Perhaps someday he will feel he can risk sharing anger or sadness with us as well.

I have noticed in other adopted children also that they seem to overreact to physical pain and underreact to other emotional stimuli. If we communicate that we want the kids to "buck up" and be brave I think we lose a valuable bonding opportunity. Letting our child know that we care enough about his pain to hold him, get band-aids, and rock him until his headache goes away can do a great deal to build attachment.

I wonder if these children have seen so much of life and experienced so much sorrow, so much illness and death that in their minds a simple headache may not seem so simple. A sprained ankle might make them fear losing a limb. There seems to be incredible anxiety that goes along with illness and injury in these young minds.

About a month after I returned from Ethiopia I became quite sick, with a fever and severe abdominal pain. Eventually we found out I had come down with a case of hepatitis A. On one of the early days of my illness I was lying in bed with a hundred and three degree fever, feeling pretty pathetic. Andrew came into the bedroom, tears streaming down his face. "Mommy," he said, "you will die!"

I assured him that we have good doctors and good medicine in America and that I wouldn't die. He replied, "Daddy died, Mommy died, Tsahaynesh died. You will die!"

Even though I really wanted to bury myself in the blankets and avoid the world I felt like I needed to be perky and cheerful to convince him that I really wouldn't die. His fear was all too real.

The first days and weeks at home are a time of adjustment for the whole family. Keep reminding yourself that this adjustment period won't last forever. Before long it might even be hard to remember not having your child in your family!

CHAPTER SIX

Medical Issues

*V*ery shortly after arriving home your child, whether adopted internationally or domestically, should have a thorough medical examination. If you are selecting a pediatrician for the first time it's a good idea to ask how much experience he or she has with adopted children. If she hasn't had much, you might ask if she is willing to learn.

There are excellent websites that list medical tests and procedures recommended for internationally adopted children. Some of these sites are *www.orphandoctor.com*, *www.adoptiondoctors.com*, and *www.comeunity.com*. It's helpful to peruse these sites to get some of your medical questions answered.

One of the issues you will need to consider is whether or not to have your child's immunizations repeated. Your child will arrive with a list of immunizations and dates. However, it is often questionable whether the vaccines met American standards. Many families choose to repeat the immunizations the child has already had.

If you choose to repeat immunizations or to complete a series that has been started, you will need to decide when to do so. Many doctors want to immunize your child immediately. You will probably want to consider your child's overall health and immune status. If he is dealing with parasites and other issues you might want to deal with these first. It seems that waiting a month or two to begin immunizations probably won't harm your child.

Immunizations can be very frightening for a child who can't communicate with you. This is another reason to consider delaying them until you build some trust between you and your child. If you decide to have the immunizations soon after your child's arrival, you might want to offer a special treat to your child immediately after the shots, regardless of whether the child has screamed or been cooperative.

One of the things you will not want to put off is having your child screened for tuberculosis. In some countries children are given a BCG vaccine that will cause them to test positive for TB, requiring a chest x-ray to determine actual TB status. This is not something you want to delay.

The doctor will want to see if your child is harboring parasites. It's a pretty safe bet that he is if he comes from a third world country. This will require you to get a stool sample from your child. The doctor will explain exactly how he wants you to collect the sample, and you need to follow the instructions carefully. It can sometimes be a challenge to get your child to cooperate! Older children can feel quite embarrassed by this procedure. This might be an appropriate time to contact some-one who speaks your child's first language and ask her to ex-plain why this needs to be done.

Sometimes several stool samples are required before the offending parasite is identified. Sometimes blood tests are re-quired. With some of our children the stool samples haven't shown any parasites, but blood tests have.

If your child arrived with serious medical issues that you need to deal with immediately, it will be a challenge to build trust with your child while he is undergoing frightening and perhaps painful procedures. It seems wise to have at least one parent remain with the child constantly.

Undergoing medical procedures can play a significant role in the bonding process. Rebekah came to us with a repaired cleft lip and unrepaired cleft palate. A few months after her arrival she had cleft palate surgery. It was quite painful and of course she couldn't talk for several days afterwards. We devel-oped our own method of communication with gestures and hand signals. As I lovingly cared for her following this and several other surgeries her trust in me grew. Each time she awoke from surgery I had a special present waiting for her. Once she received a ring for which she had been hoping. She told me later it almost made the surgery worthwhile!

We lived in Taiwan as missionaries at the time we adopted Rebekah. When she was seven she had surgery that required bone to be grafted from her hip to her gum line. Although her mouth was sore, her hip hurt even worse.

We flew from our home in southern Taiwan to Taipei, the capital in the north, so Rebekah could be operated on by the best surgeon available. We remained in the hospital about thirty-six hours after surgery and then were discharged. Because Rebekah's hip was too painful for her to walk, I had to carry her in addition to our two bags. We made it into the taxi without too much trouble, and arrived at the airport to fly back to Kaohsiung. Our progress through the terminal must have been amusing. I set down our bags (I know, you're never supposed to leave your bag unattended, but this was a few years ago!) and carried Rebekah twenty feet to a chair. Then I left her and ran back for the bags. I carried the bags about twenty feet ahead of her, then ran back for Rebekah. I continued like this throughout a very large terminal, constantly looking around for a friendly soul who might help or a spare wheelchair. Neither materialized, so we continued our back and forth progress.

Then it was time to board the plane. The stewardess told me to take the bags on and then go back for Rebekah. This I did, feeling a bit frantic at having her out of my sight.

Eventually we made it to Kaohsiung, repeated the trip through a second airport, hailed a taxi and made it home to where Steve was watching the other children. I vowed I would plan differently for future surgeries.

Difficult as this experience was, Rebekah later said to me, "You love me, Mommy. You carried me. You helped me not hurt. Thank you." I believe strongly that difficult medical situations can play a large part in bonding us with our children.

Deborah requires surgery at least once a year. The bones in her arm stubs grow as she grows but the skin and tissue around them don't stretch, so she needs to have the bones trimmed back. We have had very good experiences with Shriners Hospital for Children. They are very child-friendly and make it a point to make parents feel they are very much a part of their child's care team. Deborah says a hospital stay at Shriners is almost as good as summer camp, with a bit of pain thrown in.

As with Rebekah, I believe that a significant part of our bonding with Deborah has been through experiencing her hospital stays together. I always sleep in her room with her and Steve always makes sure that he is in her room when she awakes from surgery. Because Deborah has frequent surgeries the staff knows her well and she is normally a cheerful patient, encouraging the other children who are recovering. Her hospital stays have created many fond memories for us.

I mentioned previously that John rarely shows much emotion unless he is in physical pain. We felt that we made a breakthrough into his inner world once relating to his eye. We heard of a very young boy whose vision had been improved tremendously by a surgeon in our area. We were hopeful that he might be able to help John as well.

We didn't want to raise John's hopes only to dash them again, so we carefully explained that we were going to take him to a doctor who would tell us if he might be able to help him see a little better. John is a very bright boy with acute hearing, and he tends to learn about what is going on by eavesdropping on conversations around him. Apparently he heard some of our discussions and began to dream of clear vision.

Unfortunately the visit was not promising. The surgeon explained that eyes begin to age when we are only six years old, and since John was ten even if the surgery was done perfectly John's brain probably wouldn't realize what had happened and his vision wouldn't improve. Because John has only one eye we didn't want to risk eliminating the tiny bit of vision that he has. We asked the surgeon what he would do if John were his son, and he said he wouldn't take the risk.

John heard our conversation, but Steve wanted to be sure that he understood so he carefully explained to him why the doctor didn't think we should try. Tears streamed down John's face and he whispered, "I wanted to be able to drive."

We took John out for Indian food and talked with him for quite awhile, explaining that it was all right to feel disappointed. It was another example to us of how physical issues can help a child open up and be vulnerable.

I encourage you to use your child's medical procedures as opportunities to comfort your child, assure her of your love and let her know she can count on your support.

CHAPTER SEVEN

Practical Questions You'll Need to Consider

YOUR CHILD'S NAME

Whether or not to keep your child's name is very controversial and something to which you will need to give careful thought. Many people feel strongly that your child's name was a gift from her birthparents and the only thing she can keep from her past. They feel it is part of your child's heritage.

This is certainly a valid argument and needs to be taken into consideration. We want our children to know that we value their past and all that transpired in the time before they were in our family.

There are a couple of issues to consider, however. First, in many cases a child adopted internationally wasn't given his name by his birthparents. For example, most children in Chinese orphanages are given their surname based on the year in which they arrive at the orphanage. The second character of their name is typically given by workers in the orphanage. Rebekah's Chinese name is "Lee Bo," and all the girls who arrived at her orphanage during 1989 were given the character "Lee." So this is part of her Chinese heritage, but not something that was specifically given her by her birthparents.

Deborah's Russian name is "Mariana." We were told that she was given this name by nurses in the hospital where she spent the first year of her life, and that they named her after a character in a Brazilian soap opera. We've been told that Mariana is an unusual Russian name.

Our adopted sons, however, were both named by their birthparents. John's Indian name is "Abhilash," and Andrew's Ethiopian name is "Fikadu."

Our odyssey in naming our children may be helpful to you as you consider how you want to handle this issue. There were unique issues to consider with each child, but in the end we followed the same pattern with each.

When we adopted Rebekah we lived in Taiwan. All of us had American names and Chinese names. The children used their Chinese names in Chinese class at school, and we adults used our Chinese names to conduct official business, as well as to identify ourselves to our Chinese neighbors and friends. We all had the surname "Gao," and then we each had a two character given name. My Chinese name, for example, is Gao Mei Shwei. Gao means tall, which I'm certainly not, and Mei Shwei means Beautiful Snow.

It was easy to decide that our new daughter would also have a Chinese name and an American name. Because

Rebekah had just a two character name from her orphanage, we added our Chinese surname and her Chinese name became Gao Lee Bo.

Our birth children have biblical names. We like to name the children for a biblical character that can serve as a role model for them. We wanted to do the same for our new daughter. The biblical Rebekah had to leave her home, family and country and travel to a new home, family and country. Scripture makes it clear that Rebekah was loved by Isaac, her new husband. We wanted our daughter, also leaving her home and country, to also know that she was loved.

We wanted to keep part of Rebekah's Chinese name in her American name, so she became Rebekah Lee Gardner.

When we adopted Deborah we still lived in Taiwan so she, too, had a Chinese name. Additionally, because of Deborah's physical challenges Steve felt that she needed to be named after a strong woman, so we determined to name her after the only woman judge in Scripture, and she became Deborah Mariana Gardner.

After we returned to the States we adopted John. Because of his severe vision limitations we felt he needed a very simple name to ease his writing challenges. Additionally we wanted him to have a strong role model, and thus named him after John the Baptist. The initials for John Abhilash Gardner are JAG, and John enjoys being called "jaguar" as a nickname.

Fikadu is a fairly common Ethiopian name, but we were concerned that American children would change the vowel sounds and create a name that would be impolite. Andrew was a familiar name to him, although in Ethiopia this apostle is called Andreas. Because we have a son named Peter it seemed appropriate to name another son after Peter's brother. Thus Fikadu became Andrew Fikadu Gardner.

Dinah was named by the nuns at her Catholic orphanage who give the unnamed babies biblical names when they arrive. Since Susannah, Rebekah and Deborah all have biblical names ending in "ah," Dinah's name fit the pattern. We decided we would keep it as her first name and gave her a middle name that was very meaningful to us.

Andrew had cared for his little sister, Tsahaynesh, by himself for several months after their parents died. We were eager to welcome Andrew Fikadu and Leah Tsahaynesh into our home. However, just as our papers were ready to go to court we received news that Tsahaynesh had died. Steve flew to Ethiopia to be with Andrew and assure him we were committed to him and still planned to adopt him.

Andrew told Steve that he still would like a little sister. The only little girl available at that time was a tiny, frail premature baby who had not been expected to live. Six months of age at the time of Steve's visit, she couldn't roll over or sit up and she neither smiled nor made any sounds during the several hours he spent with her. Still, her eyes were alert and she didn't seem to miss anything going on around her.

Because of Andrew's desire for a little sister and the fact that this child was the only one available at that moment in time, we felt she was the one the Lord had for us.

In the book of Job, his children die for no apparent reason. God doesn't owe him an explanation for why this happened. But at the end of the book God blesses Job with ten more children, including three daughters. Interestingly, we are not told the names of the sons, but we are told the names of the daughters, and are told that they were given an inheritance with their brothers, which was quite unusual.

This was a very special parallel to us, since our little Tsahaynesh had also died for no apparent reason and the Lord blessed us with another baby. Keziah was one of Job's daughters, and Dinah Keziah is a special reminder of the Lord's faithfulness when things happen that we don't understand.

Our children have told us they like their names, and they very much like having their original names as their middle names. It truly does provide a link to their past.

Additionally, because several of our adopted children have obvious physical challenges, we wanted to simplify their lives by giving them fairly common American names. We knew our children would stand out from the crowd due to their physical differences and their status as ethnic minorities. We didn't want to make them even more noticeable because of unusual names.

Perhaps as you consider the many reasons we named our children as we did you will be helped to decide what you want to do about your child's name. Some families keep their child's original name as the first name and add a meaningful name as the middle name. Other families name their adopted child after a special family member or friend, and that becomes a new part of the child's life story.

Whatever you decide, there are certain to be friends and family who will disagree with your choice. Nevertheless, the choice is yours and you should make a decision with which you feel comfortable. You're the one who will live with this child and her name. Do what feels right to you.

KEEPING YOUR CHILD'S LANGUAGE

Many families are hopeful that they will be able to help their child keep his first language. It seems that it will be valuable to the child to be bilingual and it will be another connection to his roots.

There are various methods of doing this. In many cities there are Saturday or evening classes where Chinese and Russian children are exposed to their first language each week. Depending on the child's age when she arrived in America and the extent to which she spoke her first language, this may help her maintain her skills.

Some families have friends who speak their child's first language, and arrange for these friends to talk with their children regularly.

There are also language learning tools, such as the Rosetta Stone program, which help children maintain their first language.

There are other issues to consider when deciding how much effort to put into maintaining language skills. Children who leave their birth country before the age of three or four will have very limited language skills. In order to be bilingual they aren't maintaining their first language as much as they are learning it for the first time. This may require more time and effort than a family is willing to devote. Additionally, the child may learn to speak his birth country's language, but reading and writing are much more complex. A family needs to decide to what extent they want their child to have these skills.

Children adopted at elementary school ages or older probably have excellent spoken language skills and may be able to read and write. It might be valuable to help your child keep these skills.

Most children lose their first language within about six months of being adopted unless extensive effort is made to help them keep these skills. It's an interesting phenomenon that the child is losing her first language at the same time she is trying to acquire a new language. Six months isn't enough time to learn English, so there is a difficult period where she can no longer speak her first language and can't communicate well in English either. (1)

We have seen some interesting patterns as our older children have joined our family. Some children are very eager to identify with our family and apparently don't want to seem different. Deborah spoke excellent Russian at the time we adopted her, but avoided Russians to whom she was introduced and refused to talk with them. As we expected, within several months she had lost her ability to speak Russian. After a few years she had become very proud of being Russian and was eager to speak with Russians she met, but was no longer able to do so. We plan to enroll her in classes at a local Russian church this fall and anticipate she will relearn Russian rather quickly since she is highly motivated to do so.

When John came home at age nine he had already learned two languages, one from the tribal area in which he had lived until he was six years old and the other the primary language of his Indian state, which was spoken at the orphanage. His best orphanage friend, who spoke the same two languages, had been adopted by a family in Tennessee, and we encouraged them to talk on the phone often.

Within a very short time we noticed that the boys carried on most of their conversations in English. "John," we asked, "why don't you speak in your Orissa language?"

He pondered this for awhile, and then told us that he and his friend had had many experiences in America that they hadn't had in India and they didn't know the words in their first languages for the things they had experienced here. "It's much easier for us to speak English to each other," he said.

Well! So much for helping him keep his languages.

When children are learning English they often put so much effort into acquiring their new language that their first language slides. For children who have difficulty acquiring English language skills, efforts to maintain their first language may slow down their progress.

Some fortunate children have siblings who were also adopted from their birth country. The children can speak their first language together and speak English with their other family members. The downside of this may be that, because the children can speak their first language easily, they won't feel a strong need to learn English and their English language acquisition may be slower.

Each family needs to consider how important it is to them that their child maintain some level of fluency in his first language.

DETERMINING YOUR CHILD'S AGE

In American culture age is very important. It affects when children start school, get their driver's licenses, and can vote. Years later it affects when retirees can begin to collect social security payments. But in many countries, such as India and Ethiopia, age is unimportant and birth records are typically unavailable. Your child must have a birth date listed on her passport, so normally orphanage officials estimate a birth date.

In many cases this estimated date is off by a year or two. Sometimes it's wrong by three or four years. This can often be attributed to the fact that the younger a child, the better her chances of being adopted. Caregivers probably aren't intentionally deceitful, but if they think a child is somewhere between eight and ten years old, they will likely select a birth date saying the child is the youngest age possible.

There are interesting ramifications of this. Often families place a newly adopted child a year behind where his age would normally place him in school. If the child is actually two years older than his estimated age, this places him with classmates three years younger than him. While perhaps not important when a child is considered six or seven, this can be significant when the child is twelve or thirteen.

Our son John was estimated to be nine years old when we adopted him, and in nearly every way that estimate seemed appropriate. The one contrary piece of evidence was that he already had his twelve year molars. We placed him in third grade, one year behind his estimated age. He fit in very well with the children socially and physically, and within a couple of years had nearly caught up with them academically.

But suddenly, at the end of fifth grade, when John was supposed to be twelve, he began to grow a moustache, shoot up in height and develop physically in many other ways. Rather than twelve, he is probably closer to fourteen years old. Yet socially he fits in very well with his eleven and twelve year old peers. Because John is a very gentle, rather naïve child this is probably still an acceptable placement for him.

It's challenging to have a child go through puberty several years before his classmates. This is one reason it is important to try to determine a fairly accurate age for your child before making schooling decisions.

Some of our friends faced the opposite problem. When their son Nathan arrived home from India his paperwork said he was eight years old. Yet he was very small and immature and still had some baby teeth. The Dingfields decided to give him some time to catch up, and legally lowered his age by two years. Nearly three years have gone by, and it seems that this was a good decision. Nathan fits in very well with his peers based on his new age.

To help with determining your child's age you can look at all the available paperwork on her case and compare dates with other things you know about your child's history, such as when she arrived in her orphanage. You can ask an older child questions, such as how long he lived with his grandparents.

He may not know for sure, but he might remember holidays and other significant events that will give clues. You can have a dentist examine your child to see which teeth and molars she has. A doctor can order a bone scan, which will be another clue.

How old does your child consider herself to be? How did she come up with that age? Then take all these clues and, together with your pediatrician, determine which age seems most appropriate.

When you finalize your child's adoption in the States, or readopt if the adoption was finalized overseas, you can legally change your child's age as part of the paperwork process.

Notes

1. See *www.hanen.org* for additional information on language acquisition, language delays and an interesting theory called subtractive bilingualism.

CHAPTER EIGHT

Birthparent Issues

THE ROLE OF
BIRTHPARENTS

*M*any families are confused about what role birthparents should have in their child's life. Sometimes it seems like it would be easier to forget all about them and let your family be like any other family. But that would deny huge aspects of your child's life and deny all of you the opportunity to learn about and perhaps meet some incredible people.

We don't need to be afraid of our children's birthparents. You are your child's parents, you are building a strong bond with your child, and your child can love you deeply and love his birthparents, too. It's not either/or.

We have very interesting discussions about birthparents in our home. First, it always intrigues me that the children talk about their birth moms frequently, but most of them rarely mention their birth dads. I'm not sure why that is. Perhaps there is something about the relationship between a mother and child that the children innately understand.

Additionally, we don't usually use the terms "birth parent," "birth mom," and "birth dad." Because some of our children spent several years with their first parents, we usually refer to them as Rebekah's Chinese mother, or Andrew's Ethiopian dad. We want to acknowledge that their first parents did more, in many cases, than simply give them birth. In some families, where there is communication between the adoptive family and the birth parents, children call the birth parents titles such as "Mama Ashley" or "Daddy Joe."

Our three adopted daughters didn't know their birth mothers. The girls were all abandoned within the first week of their lives. We know varying degrees of information about their birth mothers, and it affects the girls' feelings quite a bit.

Rebekah was abandoned as an infant in China, likely a victim of the One Child policy along with hundreds of thousands of other girls. The fact that she had a cleft lip and palate may have also been a factor. Rebekah longs more than any of our other children to know something about her birth mother. She regularly ponders which of her characteristics may have come from her Chinese mother, and claims that she would give up every birthday present for the rest of her life if she could just meet her Chinese mother once. Unfortunately, even if we had unlimited resources there would be no way to track down Bek's Chinese mom.

Rebekah has a very tender heart and a large part of her desire to meet her Chinese mother has to do with her desire to share the Gospel with her. Rebekah desperately wants her Chinese mother to learn of the Lord's love for her. Through many conversations we have determined that perhaps a missionary or a Chinese Christian might befriend Rebekah's Chinese mom and lead her to the Lord. Rebekah prays about this faithfully, and we trust the Lord to answer her prayers and hope that she will meet her Chinese mother in heaven.

Deborah's birth parents refused to take her home from the hospital when they saw her physical abnormalities. This has resulted in some bitterness in Deborah because she feels that a mother should love her child no matter what. We know the names of Deborah's birth parents, and she typically refers to them by their first names rather than as her birth parents. Deborah toys with the idea of trying to contact her Russian mother in a few years. She dreams of standing in front of her, beautiful and capable, and seeing if her Russian mother would be more accepting of her.

Of all our children, Deborah has the clearest understanding of how the Lord works in adoption. She regularly tells people that if she had stayed in Russia she knows that she wouldn't have had the opportunity to have such good medical care, excellent schooling, and opportunities to be with other child amputees. She says she wonders if she would have learned about the Lord in Russia, and says she doesn't think she would be as smiley as she is if she had stayed there. "I know the Lord can use hard things to have good endings," Deborah says. "I'm so glad to be in America with my fun family and to know the Lord."

Dinah is only eleven months old so obviously our conversations about her Ethiopian mother are one-sided. I tell Dinah that her young, unwed birth mother loved her very much. We know that because she chose to give her life rather than to abort her. I wonder if her birth mother might have been the same age as one of our teenagers. I can imagine the fear and shame my daughter might feel in a similar situation, and I hope she would be as brave as Dinah's mom and give her child life. I want to help Dinah appreciate her Ethiopian mother's love and courage.

Our two adopted sons both lived with their birth mothers for several years, so they have very different perceptions of their birth parents than our daughters do. John and Andrew are both remarkable young men, and I tell them regularly that I wish I could have met their birth mothers. I would have felt honored to be their friend. They must have been incredible women to have raised such bright, resourceful, resilient young boys.

John's Indian father died before he was born, and he lived with his Indian mother in a remote mountainous village in India until he was six or seven years old. He remembers lying on the dirt floor of their hut, wrapped in a blanket with his Indian mom. Obviously she was a kind and loving woman. He tells stories of her working in the field all day to get some rice or vegetables, preparing the food outside their hut, and then offering it to John and his brother, claiming that she wasn't hungry for her share so that there would be more for them.

Apparently John was born with normal vision, but at a very young age contracted an infection in his eyes. One of the eyes was so painful that it was removed, leaving an empty eye socket. The other eye was so infected that John was left with extremely limited vision.

In his tiny, remote village there was little a blind child could do. He recalls spending most of his days sitting on a small stool outside their hut. As the years went by his mother apparently became quite ill, perhaps with tuberculosis, and spent a great deal of time lying on a blanket outside the hut.

Eventually, perhaps because she felt that she was dying, John's Indian mother took his brother and him to a small mountain orphanage. The person in charge wouldn't let John's brother stay, feeling he was too old and would run away. So John was left there alone, and he tells us of the utter despair and loneliness he felt. We have a couple of pictures of him from that time, and his expression is that of a child who has lost all hope.

Yet one day, when John had been at this small orphanage for a few months, his Indian mother reappeared. John recalls that she stayed very briefly, just long enough to ensure that he was all right.

What a loving mother she was! Though very poor and ill, she made the effort to hike through the mountains to check on her special little boy. I want John to understand how much she wanted him to be safe and cared for. John is a very sweet child, and undoubtedly his Indian mother missed him terribly. And yet she put his needs before her own.

Andrew's father was killed in the war between Ethiopia and Eritrea, and his mother died of malaria a few months after Tsahaynesh was born, leaving Andrew to care for his three month old baby sister. Although he was only eight years old he figured out how to feed the baby. He took a bit of injera, the Ethiopian staple bread, and chewed it until it was very soggy. Then he took it from his mouth and placed it in Tsahaynesh' mouth. It was so soft that she was able to swallow it without difficulty. In this way he kept his little sister alive.

Andrew tells of standing outside his hut one night talking with a teenage friend. A snake slithered up and bit his friend on the foot. Andrew says the friend's eyes rolled back in his head and he fell to the ground, dead.

A night or two later Andrew walked into his hut carrying Tsahaynesh. It was very dark, and he stepped on something cold and hard. He was fairly certain that it was a snake, but didn't know whether or not he had killed it when he stepped on it. The object, whatever it was, lay between him and the doorway, so he couldn't leave the hut. He took the baby and moved as far away from the object as possible, huddling against the wall of the hut. A terror filled night passed as he hoped against hope that he and Tsahaynesh wouldn't be bitten and killed. He says he didn't sleep at all and tried to keep the baby quiet and still.

When the first light of day entered the hut Andrew saw that the object was indeed a snake, and that it was still moving slightly. He yelled, and a neighbor came running with a machete and killed the snake. It was an extremely frightening experience for a young boy to endure.

Andrew is one of the most incredible, resourceful young boys we have met, and we feel privileged to be his parents. But he wouldn't have developed those qualities without guidance from his birth parents. I tell him I would have liked his

Ethiopian mom to be my good friend. She must have been a remarkable woman.

I want my children to feel proud of their heritage, proud of their history, proud of the incredible people who gave them life and, in some cases, built amazing qualities into their lives. Yes, their birth parents may not have always made good choices. I don't mean to idolize them in any way, but want my children to feel love and respect for them.

My children know I'm their mom, the one who loves them, disciplines them, sews their school costumes and plans their birthday parties. I don't need to feel threatened by their birth mothers. I wish we could have been friends and shared the joy of pouring our lives into these incredible children.

I encourage you not to be afraid to talk freely about birth parents with your children. There may be days when your child is angry with you and announces she would rather be with her birth mom. That's o.k. There are probably days when you wish your child was with her birth mom, too! Those words and threats don't matter. The important thing is that over time you are bonding with your child, developing a stronger and stronger relationship between a real parent and a real child.

BIRTHPARENT CONTACT

This is all somewhat easy to say when we're talking about international adoption and there is very little chance the children could ever meet their birth parents. But what of domestic adoption, when the option for a meeting and other forms of contact is a very real possibility?

Because all of my children were adopted internationally I haven't personally dealt with birth parent contact. However, my father was adopted as an infant and met his birth family as a young adult. It meant a great deal to him to learn the reasons his birth family had made an adoption plan for him, and he remained in contact with his birth siblings for the rest of his life. This didn't diminish his affection for his adoptive parents. His adoptive mother lived two blocks from him for most of his adult life, and he was a faithful son to her. But knowing his history positively influenced his feelings about himself.

Additionally, my father had a disease for many years that was diagnosed as multiple sclerosis. His birth brother, who had been raised in a completely different part of the country, had the same disease. We all thought this was a very unusual coincidence since MS is not supposed to have a genetic link, and the men hadn't grown up in the same environment.

Years later, just after our daughter Susannah was born, my father's brother contacted him and said he had just found out that he had a rare genetic disease rather than multiple sclerosis, that all his daughters were carriers, and that any sons they produced had a fifty percent chance of having the disease and a twenty-five percent chance of dying in childhood.

My dad was tested and, sure enough, he had the same disease, Adrenomyeloneuropathy, and my sons had a fifty percent chance of having the childhood form, Adrenoleukodystrophy. We had the boys tested and by the grace of God they were both negative. Susannah will be tested soon to see if she is a carrier.

Later, knowing the risks, my sisters each gave birth to a son and a daughter. Their sons both tested positive, but because we know of the possibility of this disease they were able to use dietary and medicinal measures immediately to cut the risk for their boys.

The opportunity to exchange information regarding medical backgrounds is a very important argument for at least a certain degree of openness in adoption. Had my father not been in contact with his biological brother we would still think he had had multiple sclerosis and wouldn't have been able to carefully monitor my nephews' progress.

OPEN ADOPTION

For children adopted domestically and for those internationally adopted children who have the option, I think we as parents need to let our children know it's o.k. for them to wonder about their birth parents and to want to have some degree of contact. There is a huge range of meaning to open adoption. It can be as simple as exchanging letters and photos on a yearly basis through an intermediary. It can be as complex as having the birth mother and perhaps birth father actually visit in the adoptive home. I'm aware of some cases where the birth mother actually lived in the adoptive home for awhile before and shortly after the birth of the baby.

In these cases there is no mystery. The child can grow up knowing her story and doesn't have to wonder why an adoption plan was made for her. With the mystery gone and freedom to contact her birth parents occasionally, a child can feel more secure in her adoptive home.

This doesn't mean you all need to be best friends. You may really not like your child's birth parents. And they may disappoint you by not showing up for a scheduled meeting or not sending a letter at an agreed upon time. Adoptive parents disappoint birth parents, too, by not following through with things that have been agreed upon. But having a way to be in contact seems healthy for everyone involved.

WHEN TO TELL YOUR CHILD

Sometimes families who adopt a child as an infant wonder when they should tell the child that he was adopted. Certainly the family shouldn't try to keep this a secret. Too many people know, and the news is bound to be blurted out sometime.

My father was adopted as an infant and raised as an only child. This was in the 1930s, when children were commonly placed for adoption with couples who looked as much like them as possible. The goal was to make it as easy as possible for a couple to pass the child off as their birth child.

Imagine the shock he felt one day at the age of twelve, when a visiting cousin blurted out, "I know something you don't know!" and proceeded to tell him that he had been adopted. He ran inside and confronted his parents with this information. Thankfully they responded truthfully that he had indeed been adopted. However, it created quite a rift between my father and his parents throughout his teenage years, as he wondered in what other important areas they may not have been truthful with him.

Acquaintances of ours adopted a lovely little boy as an infant. When he was four years old, they pondered how to tell him that he had been adopted. I was troubled because the boy was very bright, everyone else knew he had been adopted, and it seemed only a matter of time until someone would say something in his presence that would be unsettling to him.

I told the parents of my concern, and they asked how they should tell him. The father said that it was becoming more and more difficult to talk with the boy about his life without telling a lie! This situation was very unfortunate but quite avoidable. People talk with their children regularly about their birth stories, mentioning how long they were in labor or who visited in the hospital. With adopted children the details are different, but the sharing of the stories should be the same.

We don't need to wait until children are able to understand the whole story. Just talk about it in casual conversation. For example, when talking about a pregnant friend, you can comment, "When you were in your birth mom's tummy, I wonder if you wiggled around a lot."

You can mention the thrill you felt as you were heading to the hospital or the foster home to pick up your child. You might mention the clothes you picked out and what you thought the first time you saw your child. All of this can be mentioned casually, often in the context of excitement over a friend's pregnancy or adoption plans. Your child should never remember a time when she didn't know she was adopted. It simply shouldn't come as a surprise or be something you need to sit your child down and have a major talk about.

If your child is of a different ethnic group than you, this gives another way of conversing about adoption. You can comment that her skin color is very much like her birth mother's, or that you have always admired hair like hers and are enjoying learning how to care for it.

Showing respect to a child's birth parents, whether you have the opportunity to meet them or not, shows your child that you respect his background and that there is nothing for which he needs to feel ashamed. Admittedly, some situations from which our children come are very difficult, and often children have suffered abuse of various types in their past. But none of this is our child's fault. Usually we can find something good, however small, about the birth family and give this information to our child to hold onto.

CHAPTER NINE

Setting Boundaries and Establishing Routines

One of the more troublesome problems that families often have to deal with is the difficulty many children have in submitting to their parents' authority. There is a delicate balance between helping children adjust and feel comfortable with their new lives and requiring children to learn the rules of their new home and obey their new parents.

Many children have been in charge of their own lives for quite awhile, and often feel that they did a pretty good job of it. It's hard for children who have had to make all the decisions for themselves and perhaps for younger siblings to let themselves be children again and submit to letting you be the parent.

Andrew lived with his parents and baby sister in a remote Ethiopian village, without electricity or running water. After his parents died Andrew, at age eight, cared for his sister and did a remarkably good job. For example, the people in his village gave him a bit of money. Andrew wanted to buy himself a new pair of pants because his old ones were very shabby. However, he decided that it was more important that the baby have milk. So he bought a pregnant goat, reasoning that when the baby goat was born he could milk the mother goat and feed the milk to his baby sister. Then, after the baby goat grew a bit, he could sell it and use the money to buy the pants he needed. This was incredible thinking for an eight year old boy. Most of the boys of this age that I know can't even match their own socks!

So he purchased a pregnant goat and let it graze in the field. One day he was tending some crops and keeping an eye on his goat, about a football field away. As he watched, a leopard appeared and stealthily approached his goat. He screamed, but the leopard grabbed his goat and carried it up a tree. Andrew threw himself to the ground, screaming "My money! My money!" After all, with how much can one little kid cope?

Andrew says that when the leopard left the goat carcass, he and his neighbor discovered that actually the goat was pregnant with two kids. He says he could have bought pants as well as other necessary supplies by selling both baby goats.

Having made this type of decision on his own for several months, it's obvious why it's difficult for Andrew to calmly accept our authority over him. He is very bossy, interrupts regularly to make sure we see his side of the situation, and likes nothing better than being in charge. I have to calmly remind him that I'm the mom and he needs to listen to me. It's not easy for him.

He parented himself and Tsahaynesh for so long that our goal is for him to learn to relax and be a child again. We don't want him to feel that he needs to make major decisions. We want him to learn that he can trust us to provide for him and deal with the big issues in his life for now.

Last July 4th we went to some friends' home to watch the fireworks display put on by the city. It was a wonderful evening full of friends, food and fun, and we didn't get home until nearly midnight.

The next day Andrew was tired and grumpy. Steve told him that he needed to go to bed at 8:00 that night in order to be rested the next day. Andrew became very angry and loudly said, "I Ethiopia boy! Ethiopia boy no go bed 8:00!"

Steve calmly replied, "Oh yes! Ethiopia boy will go to bed at 8:00 tonight, and Ethiopia boy will go to bed at 8:00 tomorrow night too if you don't settle down."

A few minutes later we prayed together as a family as we do every night. The other children prayed and Steve asked Andrew to pray, which he had done for several evenings. He angrily said, "I no pray English!"

Steve told him he could pray in Amharic, or he could try to pray in English. Andrew grumpily said, "Try? What is try?"

I told Andrew that he needed to go to bed immediately because he was being disrespectful. It was 7:45.

He glanced at the clock and stomped downstairs. When I went down a few minutes later to tuck John and him into their beds his head was covered with a blanket and he refused to remove it.

"I love you, Andrew. Have a good sleep! I hope you feel better tomorrow," I said, suspecting that his anger would be short-lived.

And sure enough, the next day he was the perfect child. In fact, he pointed out to everyone exactly how perfect he was. Surely a child that well-behaved wouldn't be required to go to bed at 8:00, while it was still light outside!

And so it goes, and so it goes. We assure him of our love and commitment, and sometimes he thrives on acting like a little boy only to be very bossy and controlling half an hour later.

After two months we are seeing Andrew be more and more responsive to us and obey our instructions without much argument. He still struggles a great deal when he feels that his older brothers and sisters are too bossy. It frustrates him that he is the seventh of eight children. He would very much like to be the oldest!

I tell new parents regularly that their job is to be their child's parent, not their child's best friend. You need to help your child learn boundaries and follow up with consequences for disobedience and defiance. Regardless of what age your child was when you adopted her, she is your child and, as her parent, you have the right and responsibility to follow Scriptural principles in training her, just as you would a child who was born to you.

It is appropriate to set standards for the behavior you expect in public places, such as church and stores. After you explain to your child through gestures or words where to sit, where he must be quiet, where it is not appropriate to run, and other rules you want followed, you might give your child a warning and then enforce some type of consequence for disobedience. It's not necessary to allow wild behavior just because of their age or lack of English. However, most of us tend to get involved in conversations at church or are busy with our shopping list at the store and don't pay attention to our children. It's a good idea to explain to our children the behavior we expect and then give them our attention for several weeks to make certain they follow our instructions.

When Deborah joined our family she was four years old and an absolute terror. She kicked the other children, spit at them and called them nasty Russian names. For a child without arms she did a very good job of holding her own.

She was obstinate and defiant. When we told her to do something we could count on her immediately doing the opposite. On the plane trip home from Russia Deborah fought against wearing her seatbelt. Steve calmly but firmly insisted she stay buckled. Deborah looked at him, moved her foot under his tray, and deliberately kicked, spilling his orange juice all over his lap. For a few weeks we honestly wondered if we had made a mistake in bringing her into our home.

We knew that Deborah had to learn that she could trust us. We gave her lots of affection, but also consistently dealt with her defiance in a loving but firm way. As a four year old the big move from her orphanage in Russia to our home in Taiwan was quite overwhelming. We wanted her to know that she could count on us.

Tedd Tripp, author of *Shepherding a Child's Heart*, reminds us, "As a parent you have authority because God calls you to be an authority in your child's life . . . . You may not try to shape the lives of your children as pleases you, but as pleases Him."(1)

In Genesis 18:19 (NIV) the Lord says, "I have chosen him (Abraham) so that he will direct his children and his household after him to keep the ways of the Lord by doing what is right and just . . ."(2)

We are called to be the authority in our child's life, whether that child joins our family at birth or much later in life. Scripture is our guidebook. It is fairly easy to coerce a child into complying with a parent's commands. We've all heard illustrations of a rebellious child, sent to sit in a corner, fuming, "I'm sitting down on the outside, but I'm standing up on the inside!"

What we want is not simply to control our children's behavior. We want to reach the attitudes of our child's heart. This involves, first, being faithful and wise parents ourselves. It involves carefully examining and reworking the goals we have for our children. We need to understand and embrace Biblical methods of dealing with our children.

Shepherding a Child's Heart is perhaps the best book on parenting that I have read. It is solidly Biblically based and very helpful. Other books that help us deal with our children's hearts, rather than just their behavior, are listed in the notes.(3)

We want our children to live for the glory of God. We want them to understand that a life worth living is lived under the lordship of Jesus Christ. A biblical approach to raising children involves two elements. One is rich, full communication. The other is the rod of discipline.(4)

As we implemented these methods with Deborah, it surprised and humbled all of us that her behavior began to improve quite quickly. Within three or four months she had settled down a great deal and was quite pleasant to be around. We continued to consistently set standards and enforce our expectations, while giving her lots of attention and love and talking through issues, and she is now a delightful, though still strong-willed, young woman.

I'm not speaking as an expert, just as a fellow adoptive mom. My observation is that every child and every family are unique. The time line with which one child settles in and adjusts to her new family life shouldn't be the expectation for another child. If your child's behavior is challenging, be prepared to spend a lot of time with him for awhile. Lower your standards for your home. Your child is more important than a tidy house.

Why should your child trust you more than he trusts anyone else? Sure you have the title mom or dad, but your child doesn't know you. Clear your calendar and focus on your child and family. It's easy for all of us to get pre-occupied and not give our children our full attention.

Make sure that you have fun with your child! You might need to remind yourself each day to take time to play and laugh together. When you must deal with your child's misbehavior, she'll respond better if she has a large store of fun times with you to remember. Be goofy and full of surprises. This is harder for some of us than others, but it goes a long way toward building bonds.

When your child is going through a difficult time of adjustment try to deal with issues as soon as they arise. Make your children your priority—not just the newly adopted child, but all of the kids. The first several months with a new child in your home are stressful under the best of circumstances. If things seem more difficult than you expected, try slowing down. Make sure you all get enough sleep and exercise. Most importantly, take some time each day to be quiet, talk with the Lord, and remember why you pursued adoption in the first place. Find a friend to pray with you. In most cases things really do get better as time goes on.

Notes:

1. Tedd Tripp, *Shepherding a Child's Heart* (Wapwallopen, PA: Shepherd Press, 1995), 46.
2. Ibid., 47.
3. Other books that seek to change a child's heart rather than merely his behavior include: *Peacemaking for Families*, by Ken Sande, published by Tyndale House Publishers in 2002; *The Heart of Anger*, by Lou Priolo,

published by Calvary Press in Amityville, NY, in 1997; and *War of Words*, by Paul David Tripp, published by P&R Publishing Company, Phillipsburg, New Jersey, in 2000.

4. Tedd Tripp, *Shepherding a Child's Heart* (Wapwallopen, PA: Shepherd Press, 1995), 94.

CHAPTER TEN

School Issues

EDUCATIONAL OPTIONS

One of the first decisions you will have to make for an older child relates to schooling choices. This requires careful thought, research and prayer. I realize that educational choices are very personal and families and churches can have strong opinions about these choices. However, I encourage you to investigate choices you might not normally consider. The needs of children adopted at older ages can be different than those of children who have grown up in your family. It is important to consider each child's needs individually. There is no decision that is best for every child. Prior to your child's arrival it's a good idea to research all the available options. Remember that the decision you make initially may not be the decision you will make after the first year or two. You should reevaluate your choices at least yearly. When there are several children in a family, you may make different educational choices for various children in order to meet their different needs.

Don't let well-meaning friends and relatives convince you to make a choice with which you aren't comfortable. After even a short time you know your child's needs and your own capabilities better than anyone else does.

HOMESCHOOLING

Many families choose to homeschool their new children, at least for a time. This has the advantage of allowing your child to adjust to all his new experiences at a slower pace. It can facilitate your child's bonding with you and his new siblings as you spend large portions of time together. The frustration of language learning is often easier to cope with in the family unit. It gives you time to assess your child's strengths and weaknesses both academically and socially and allows you the opportunity to let your child regress to a younger age for a time if necessary. It also allows you to concentrate on the academic areas in which your child is weak and not to overwhelm your child with too many expectations at once.

Some families feel pressured to homeschool without having the desire, resources or support to do so. You may have intentionally adopted older children so that they will be in school during much of the day, allowing you to continue with a job or other responsibilities. You may see gaps in your child's learning that you're uncertain how to bridge. Perhaps educating a child whose English skills are minimal is disconcerting to you. Your child may have physical challenges for which the public school will provide equipment that would be cost-prohibitive for you.

In adoptive families with several children the diverse needs and range of ages can be overwhelming to mothers who are also trying to adjust their schedules and lifestyle to accommodate additional children.

Remember that whatever decision you make can be re-evaluated, revised and re-visited on a regular basis.

PUBLIC SHOOL

Children adopted at an older age have special needs related to education. If adopted internationally, minimally they need to learn a new language. Quite likely they haven't received as much education as their American peers, resulting in a disparity between their chronological age and their academic age. Even if adopted domestically, their life experiences have been different than those of most American children. All of this can make it a challenge to find a good educational plan for the child.

Public law 94–142, enacted over twenty-one years ago, provides that handicapped children and adults ages three to twenty-one be educated in the "least restrictive environment" to the maximum extent appropriate, meaning that they are educated with children who are not handicapped and that special classes, separate schools or other removal of children from their regular educational environment occurs only when the severity of the handicap is such that education in regular classes cannot be achieved.

This implies several things. Although a non-English speaking child is not strictly handicapped, presumably he will be given help learning English or the opportunity to receive instruction in his or her first language. A child whose academic skills are below grade level due to inadequate schooling or lack of exposure should receive extra help to reach grade level. Children with physical issues should have the environment modified or aides provided so that they can learn along with their peers. As much of this as possible should occur in cooperation with the regular classroom.

In most cases both your child's needs and the school's plan to meet those needs will be spelled out in an Individualized Education Plan, also known as an IEP. On a yearly basis you will meet with a committee of school personnel to agree on what will be done to meet your child's needs over the next year.

The willingness with which schools comply with this law varies from state to state and city to city. Some schools will welcome your child and enjoy the challenge of designing an appropriate educational environment. Other schools may indeed design an IEP but not be careful to follow through with meeting the yearly goals. As parents it is often your responsibility to advocate for your child. Don't wait until the yearly meeting to ensure progress is being made toward the goals. If you have concerns about your child's progress, check in with your child's teacher and other school staff on a regular basis, perhaps monthly. Schools are trying to meet the needs of many children, and you don't want your child's needs to be overlooked.

CHRISTIAN AND OTHER PRIVATE SCHOOLS

Christian schools can be a wonderful learning environment for children. Caring teachers who can freely share the love of Christ with their students, Bible lessons to give your child a Biblical background, and wise faculty who deal with problems from a Scriptural perspective are wonderful gifts to give a child. However, families should carefully consider whether this is the best option for their newly adopted older child.

Although private schools are a wonderful opportunity for many children, they are usually not equipped to meet the needs of children with unusual challenges. Average and above average children typically fare well in private schools, but children whose English is quite limited, whose academic background has significant gaps, or who have physical, mental or emotional challenges may be extremely frustrated. Most private schools don't have support staff to work with children with special needs. The regular staff often doesn't have the training required to meet these diverse challenges. Additionally, the academic expectations in most private schools don't allow for the slower pace that these children may require.

Some families may feel strongly that they want their child in a Christian school. If you do, make sure that you meet with the principal and staff prior to your child's arrival and come up with an educational plan for your child. Be certain to touch base with your child's teacher weekly, perhaps even daily, at first so you can be appraised of problems and deal with them immediately. Make sure your child isn't feeling pressured to progress more quickly than is possible given all the other adjustments she is facing.

Our family's Educational Saga

We have used each of these educational options with our children. When we adopted Rebekah we were missionaries in Taiwan, teaching at Morrison Academy, a school for missionary and business children. Our initial plan was that I would resign from teaching and teach Rebekah at home. However, over our initial summer together we observed that Rebekah is a very social child. She eagerly followed her older siblings in their adventures and always wanted to be right in the middle of any activity. We decided that we would enroll her in kindergarten at Morrison and keep a close eye on her progress, since we interacted with her teacher daily at the school.

Rebekah grew a lot during that first year. Everything was new and exciting to her. She quickly adjusted to the school routine and enjoyed going each day. When first grade rolled around we hoped for another successful year. However, the first grade program was highly academic. Although there were other English as a Second Language students, we began to realize that Rebekah's issues involved more than just language learning. The deprivation of her early life had resulted in serious academic struggles. By the end of the first semester she was seriously lagging behind her classmates in her academic progress. Although the class size was small, the school wasn't designed or equipped to deal with students who couldn't keep up.

Because I had a teaching contract I needed to finish the school year. We requested that Rebekah's teacher lighten the pressure to perform academically, realizing that she would end the year far behind expectations. Rather than renew my teaching contract, the next year I kept Rebekah home. My academic goals were to teach her to read and do simple arithmetic. But more importantly I wanted to help her learn to work independently, to be able to concentrate, and to enjoy learning.

A few months before our homeschooling venture began we added Deborah to our family. Although we had been told that she was developmentally delayed, in reality she was a very bright, spunky four and a half year old. Her curiosity and fascination with life were infectious and spurred Rebekah to want to try.

Rebekah made good progress and did indeed learn to read and understand numbers during the year. Perhaps more importantly she learned to work without having me stand beside her constantly. But despite the very positive gains Rebekah made, she was frustrated that her siblings enjoyed many activities through the missionary children's school in which she was missing out. This is one of the frustrations that can be felt by families who choose various educational options for their children.

The following year we returned to the States to live. We were comfortable enrolling the other children in public school, but I was concerned about the best option for Rebekah. After lengthy discussions with the principal and Rebekah's potential teacher we decided to enroll her and communicate regularly. This has turned out to be a good decision. Throughout elementary school Rebekah was given individual help in reading, writing and math and had very concerned teachers who were willing to keep in close contact with us. Now in middle school, Rebekah is no longer receiving special help. In regular classes, she normally receives Bs, with an occasional A or C.

She plays in the school band, participates in sports and enjoys reading for pleasure. We continue to evaluate the best educational option for her each year.

We enrolled Deborah in public kindergarten upon our return from Taiwan. She had been with our family just over a year, and surprisingly her English was nearly flawless. On the kindergarten entrance test she scored on the high end of a child who had been born and raised in the United States. Obviously her educational needs were going to be different than Rebekah's.

More than academics, we were concerned about how the school would manage Deborah's physical challenges. The kindergarten curriculum normally includes a great deal of cutting and other fine motor tasks. Obviously the majority of these would not be possible for Deborah. In the early years of her schooling we had other concerns, including toileting and lunch time issues.

The first school she attended attempted to solve these issues by hiring a full-time aide to assist Deborah. Although their intentions were good, we didn't want Deb to feel that she was so "disabled" that she couldn't learn to work independently. We requested that the aide assist other children as well and not simply hover over Deborah.

After two years we moved when Steve accepted a pastoral position. Across the street from our new home is a public elementary school that has gone far beyond what was required of them in order to meet the needs of our children. Rather than hiring an aide to help Deborah, their philosophy has been to modify the environment so that she can function independently. Among other things, they modified a bathroom for her use, installed an alternate type of doorknob on doors she would use, and provided her with a desk with a different design than those used by the other students so she could reach the contents. They have applied for a grant to get her a voice activated computer and she is expected to produce high-quality work in keeping with her abilities. Our choice of public school for Deborah has partly been determined by the assistive technology the school is able to provide Deborah that we couldn't provide on our own. Additionally, she sees herself as completely normal as she is required to creatively figure out ways to fulfill assignments.

By the time we adopted John we had a very good working relationship with the elementary school staff. When we told them we were considering adopting a child with extreme vision limitations they were undaunted. They assured us that they have a vision specialist who would work with him regularly. John arrived at age nine having had no education. We enrolled him a grade behind his age and the school arranged for tutors in reading and math. John was eager to learn and within three years has nearly caught up with his classmates. Besides daily work with a vision specialist, the school provided ESL help and resource room assistance and purchased numerous tools for John's use. These ranged from equipment that magnified printed materials to enable him to see them to soccer and basketballs with bells inside so he could participate in P.E. classes.

Our very positive public school experiences may not necessarily be what your family will experience if you choose this option.

Schooling choices are very personal decisions. I encourage families to consider the needs each child presents, thoroughly investigate local options, and realize that choices can be changed from year to year. Most important is not to abdicate your role as the one ultimately responsible for your child's education. No matter what you choose, stay involved and follow through with regular communication.

SCHOOL ASSIGNMENTS AFFECTED BY ADOPTION

There are other school issues related to adoption of which you should be aware. Quite often children are requested to bring in baby pictures, either as part of an "All About Me" project or so that the class can guess which baby picture is each classmate. For children who arrive in their family past babyhood this can not only be very frustrating but can also remind them of the losses they've had in their lives. Our earliest picture of Andrew is from age eight. It's easy for him to feel like he missed out on most of his childhood. Baby picture assignments can reinforce this sense of loss.

Additionally, if your child is the only one of his or her ethnic group in the class the child can feel that the whole project is ridiculous. "What's the point of this?" sighed Rebekah. "Everyone knows I'm the only Chinese girl in my class."

This can be a sensitive issue for foster children as well. Our eleven year old foster son came to us with five pictures of his life, none of which had been taken before he was seven years old. Of course foster families are encouraged to create lifebooks for the children in their care, but some children move so frequently that this simply doesn't happen.

Family trees are another difficult assignment for adopted children. The easiest solution is for the child to simply use the information of her adopted family. But that denies a big part of our child's heritage. When Deborah was given a family tree assignment last year she struggled over what to do. She is very proud of her Russian roots and wanted to acknowledge them in some way. Eventually she came up with a clever solution.

She drew a large tree and wrote the names of her relatives through Steve's and my families. Then she drew a smaller tree to the side and wrote as much information as she could find about her Russian family. We know her birth parents' names, and because of Russian patronymics we could extrapolate her Russian grandfathers' names.

After completing this Deborah decided to make a tree for Rebekah and one for John as well. On each tree she put all the information we have about their birth families, and then she drew lines connecting each of the small trees to the large tree, showing that each of the adopted children was grafted in to the adoptive family. "There!" she exclaimed proudly when done. "I don't have just a family tree! I have a family orchard!"

We felt this was a very good solution to the family tree assignment, and her teacher was pleased as well. I think it also demonstrated to the teacher that she could encourage children from non-traditional backgrounds to visually show their roots if they choose to do so.

Deborah's class also studied the meaning of names, and each child was to research the meaning of their family name as well as the meaning of their first and middle names and why they were given those names. This was a very interesting assignment and undoubtedly opened up many conversations in families.

In Deborah's case, however, she wasn't certain if she wanted to research her American name or her Russian name. In the end she decided to do twice the work and research both. After completing the assignment twice, she sighed and said, "I'm kind of a complicated person!" She was very proud of her research and enjoyed sharing the story of both of her names with her classmates.

Many of these activities were appropriate and fun several years ago when most children grew up in their families of origin and most adoptions were of domestic infants. Teachers might remember these projects fondly from their own childhoods, and may benefit from gentle explanations of why they aren't always appropriate any longer. Often teachers are willing to come up with an alternate, more appropriate assignment. If you do need to ask for assignment modification you might want to have an alternative to suggest.

There are less obvious assignments that can bring up feelings of loss for adopted children. In Rebekah's seventh grade science class the students were required to chart their weight at six month intervals, beginning with their weight at birth. Since we didn't have weights for the first six years of Rebekah's life she asked her teacher if she could start with her weight at six years of age. Not really understanding her reason for this request, he told her to make up weights for those missing years. She came home quite distraught, feeling like the first six years of her life hadn't mattered. We called the teacher, explained her feelings, and she was allowed to begin with her weight at age six. Keeping communication open with teachers can eliminate a lot of problems.

CLASSMATES' PERCEPTION OF ADOPTION

When Rebekah was in fourth grade I delivered cupcakes to her classroom on her birthday. I heard the boy sitting next to her ask, "Who's that lady?"

Rebekah responded, "My mom!"

"She doesn't look like you," said the boy. "How can she be your mom?"

"My parents adopted me," replied Rebekah.

Obviously adoption was pretty much a foreign concept to this young man. "Didn't your real mom want you?" he asked.

"She did, but she didn't know how to take care of me because I have a cleft palate," said Rebekah.

"Wow," he said. "Isn't it weird to live with people who aren't really your family?"

"They are my family. You just don't get it," responded Rebekah, ending the conversation.

Many children aren't familiar with or comfortable with the idea of adoption, and tend to wonder why their friend's "real parents" didn't want them. We can take opportunities to share with our children's classmates, informally or with the whole class, what adoption means and typical reasons children need new families. National Adoption Month is November, and teachers may be willing to let you make a presentation about adoption or read an appropriate book to the class.

Deborah and John are in the same grade in school. Deborah is a very fair-skinned Russian and John is a very dark-skinned East Indian. They like to say that they're twins. More than once their classmates have scoffed at them, "You aren't even brother and sister. How could you be twins?"

Deborah responds with a twinkle in her eye, "Well, we're not identical. He's a boy and I'm a girl!" Then she goes on to explain that they are, indeed, brother and sister.

As parents we need to be aware that many of our children's peers don't see adoption as positive, but instead perceive that it was the result of our child being rejected by his or her birth family. I have often noticed children watching me interact with my adopted children, and I know they are trying to understand our relationship. I want them to see that I am my children's mom in every sense of the word.

We don't need to get on a soapbox about adoption, but quietly use opportunities that arise to show that adoption can be very positive for everyone involved.

CHAPTER ELEVEN

Spiritual Development

⚜

For many of us, one of the primary reasons that we adopt is to give our child the opportunity to learn about the Lord and accept Him as savior. Adoption can be a form of evangelism. Statistics show that well over seventy percent of Christians accept the Lord before the age of twelve. Childhood is clearly a time when hearts are ripe.

It's easier to send money and gifts to orphanages than to actually bring needy children into our homes. Yet when a child is adopted into a loving Christian family it is quite likely that he or she will accept Christ. Adoption is, perhaps, the longest ministry commitment possible.

And yet when we bring an older child into our home we sometimes wonder how to begin to share Biblical truths with him.

This can be complicated if we adopt a child whose religious background is different than ours. John spent three years in a Hindu orphanage, and we're not certain what exposure he had to religion prior to that time. He eagerly participated in spiritual activities with us and joined in willingly at church and in devotion times at home.

One night, though, as I was tucking him into bed he asked, "Why do you tell me there is one God and in India they told me there are many gods?"

This was an excellent question that showed us that he was attempting to process all that he was being told. It was also a difficult question to answer, because we didn't want to imply that his caregivers in India were foolish or attempting to confuse him.

We asked John how God talks to us and where we learn about Jesus. He said in the Bible. We explained to him that many people don't have Bibles and so they try to think of what makes sense to them about how the world works.

As John has gotten older we have explained to him that many people choose not to believe what is in the Bible, because then they would feel convicted to obey God and submit to Him. We have also told him that many people are taught by their parents and teachers to believe something other than what is in the Bible.

These issues that we discuss with children adopted at older ages are really not so different from those we must discuss with all of our children. Our goal is for our children to make their relationship with the Lord personal, and not merely to believe because that is how they have been raised. We want John and the others to see the Lord at work so clearly that they are delighted to be His child. But this doesn't happen automatically, even with children who have been in our family since birth. We must be available to answer questions and model a genuine walk with the Lord.

It gave us great joy when John accepted Christ as his Savior on his one year anniversary of joining our family. As with other young children, he continues to learn and grow in his Christian faith.

Attending church as a family is a good starting point for training your child in spiritual matters. However, you can't assume that an older child will get the big picture of Scripture just by attending Sunday School and church. We have discovered that many of the common Bible stories children are taught in preschool and early elementary school are not taught regularly in older grades. Instead, the lessons often deal with applying a principle to the children's lives.

Although this is also important, there is a lot of value in having the children know Bible stories as well. We have found that the children enjoy it when we read a Bible story book to them, even when they are eleven or twelve years old. It helps them see how the stories in the Bible all tie together and point to Christ.

The children enjoy being read to, and a peaceful family time reading Bible stories, discussing Biblical truth and praying together is my favorite way to end the day. We don't manage to do this every day, but try to make time several days a week.

We've also found that the children enjoy having their own Bibles, even before they can read them. There is a plethora of children's Bibles available and you can easily find something appropriate at a Christian bookstore.

Talk about the Lord as you go about your daily activities. When you see a beautiful rainbow you can discuss why God made it. Watching bugs provides the opportunity to discuss creation, while busy ants give us the chance to discuss diligence. It's fun when the children are familiar enough with the Bible that you can say, "That reminds me of . . ." and discuss a story you have recently read.

As we are told in Deuteronomy 6:6 and 7, "And these words, which I am commanding you today, shall be on your heart; and you shall teach them diligently to your sons and shall talk of them when you sit in your house and when you walk by the way and when you lie down and when you rise up." We should talk about the Lord, His attributes and His word very matter-of-factly with our children. Our prayer is that they will see it as such a natural part of life that they will embrace this faith as their own.

CHAPTER TWELVE

Life as an Adoptive Family

TELLING OTHERS YOUR CHILD'S HISTORY

You need to decide how much of your child's history you want to share with others, including your family members. This is another of those issues about which there are very strong feelings.

Some people are adamant that their child's story is his alone, and that it is up to the child to decide how much of his story he wants to share with others. Several years ago we were getting to know a couple who had two children, a birth daughter and an adopted son. The boy was beautiful, with dark hair and eyes and slightly tanned skin. My husband casually asked about his ethnic background, and the parents said, "Oh, that's his story. We don't want to share his personal information."

We were somewhat taken aback. True, we really had no need to know this information, but it didn't seem excessively private. It was more along the lines of asking a friend where his daughter's red hair came from, when both parents are brunette. To us it seemed that this is the type of casual conversation friends have, demonstrating an interest in our friends' children.

Since then we have learned that some people feel very strongly that all details about their child's past are private. I've read articles in adoption magazines encouraging adoptive parents to respond to questions by saying something like, "Why do you want to know?" Then the parents can determine if the inquirer is merely curious or has a genuine reason for wanting the information.

I don't think there is one solution for every situation. People we run into at a restaurant or grocery store are probably just curious about our child and family and we can give them a general response. Sometimes they might be interested for personal reasons, though, and if we have the time we should be prepared to talk a bit more.

But what of friends and family who want to know personal details of our child's birth story and early life? Personally, in most cases I don't think we need to be highly secretive of these matters. For example, to share that Dinah was born to an unwed teenage mother doesn't seem too personal to me. Perhaps learning this will help a young girl in a similar situation consider a decision she may not have thought about previously, and realize that making an adoption plan for her baby can be a loving choice. I don't think anyone would look at Dinah differently once they knew her birth story.

There are some situations, however, that would wisely not be shared. Recently I was asked to help find a family for a baby boy born in an incestuous relationship between a four-teen year old girl and her seventeen year old brother. This information seems very personal and I would not share it freely. If people were aware of the baby's background it very well might affect their interaction with him. They might constantly be looking for any signs of his background in his appearance or behavior.

Whether or not to share this type of information with extended family and close friends can be difficult to decide. If you are determined that you want the information to remain secret you are giving up control of that if you share the information with even one person. You really don't know if the person you share with will choose to share with just one other person, and so on.

A good rule of thumb is that you will not tell anyone else something about your child that your child doesn't already know. You don't want your child to accidentally find out difficult things about her past. If the information is something you would feel comfortable having people talk about in front of your child, it is probably not too personal to share.

CELEBRATING HOLIDAYS

Most of our children come from rather simple backgrounds. If they celebrated Christmas in their orphanage it may have involved something as simple as cake and soda pop. If the children were in foster care they may have had more elaborate celebrations, but quite possibly they also had fairly simple holidays.

When John joined our family at nine years of age we wondered how we could celebrate Christmas without overwhelming him. He wasn't familiar with the holiday at all, and we knew that a typical American Christmas would be too much for him.

We talked with our five other children and asked them if they would be willing to simplify our Christmas celebration. We suggested that each child would receive one gift from Steve and me and that we guaranteed to make the day unforgettable.

At first the kids weren't sure about this. Although our Christmases have never been elaborate, there has always been a pile of gifts simply due to the size of our family. Then one by one the kids came to us and said they were willing to try.

The children contacted their relatives and asked them to donate money rather than send gifts. Then the kids got a catalog from Partners International and selected gifts to be sent around the world with this money. The children very much enjoyed selecting these gifts. Peter used his money to purchase a bicycle for an evangelist in China. Aaron paid for part of a well in India. Susannah bought some piglets for a farm family in Viet Nam. Rebekah was pleased to be able to use her money to send Bibles to China. John chose to send Bibles to India, and Deborah paid for Christian literature for Russia. It was a very special experience and the children felt they really were making a difference for other families around the world.

A couple of days before Christmas I prepared hot cider for everyone and put it in cups with lids to prevent spilling. I placed these cups in the van, along with pillows and quilts. We had the children get ready for bed as usual, and then instructed them to get into the van. "But we're in our pajamas!" they protested, and we assured them that's exactly what we wanted. Then we got our Golden Retriever and our black Lab and loaded them into the van as well.

When everyone was settled we drove all around the city looking for the most beautiful displays of Christmas lights that we could find. With Christmas music playing, the dogs at the kids' feet, and hot cider in their tummies it was a very memorable night. A couple of times we got out, slippers and all, and walked through displays.

Steve and I knew that, even though we didn't want Christmas to be materialistic, we wanted it to be a lot of fun. We prepared a very special gift for each child. Steve made a special box for Deborah in which she could keep all her treasures. I made a replica of a Civil War shirt for Aaron, who does Civil War reenacting. We prepared a scrapbook for Peter of all the plays he had ever been in. The other children's gifts were equally special.

Knowing it wouldn't take long to open one gift per child, we wanted to draw out the excitement. After the children went to bed on Christmas eve Steve and I took a large skein of yarn per child and unrolled them throughout the house, yard, and even through the car. We tied one end to the Christmas tree and the other end to the child's gift, hidden in some unexpected place.

On Christmas morning the children were shocked to see a spider web of yarn throughout the entire house. They gathered in the living room to be given their instructions. Steve had prepared a riddle that they had to solve in order to determine which color of yarn was for each child. After solving the riddle they began rolling up their balls of yarn as they traipsed through the house and yard. With a great deal of excitement they eventually found their gifts and gathered in the living room to share them.

John found the entire experience a great deal of fun, and commented, "Was David's ball of yarn as big as mine?" David Repsold is his good friend, and John assumed that every family found their gifts by following a trail of string!

Steve and I had purchased a few items for the whole family to enjoy, and throughout the day we would call out, "Time for a treasure hunt!" Then we'd send the kids all over the house until they eventually found a game, video or puzzle. Once they found the item we immediately used whatever it was. We found this a refreshing change from the many years when someone would open a game and we'd say, "We'll have to play that soon!" only to find that it was weeks before we did.

Later in the day we reenacted the Christmas story and went out to look at the stars, discussing how the magi knew to follow a particular star.

Finally we dragged out sleeping bags and had a giant family slumber party, complete with popcorn and hot chocolate. The cozy children declared it was absolutely the best Christmas ever and that they wanted only one present again the next year. We realized, of course, that it wasn't the number of presents that really had impressed them, but the fact that we had spent the entire day enjoying each other. For John this first Christmas experience was very special. He hadn't been overwhelmed with too much stimulation, but had been surrounded by family and love.

I'm not suggesting you imitate our celebration, but that you give serious consideration to emphasizing Christ, family and giving rather than possessions at this very hectic time of year. It doesn't matter if it's different than what everyone else is doing. Each family can build unique traditions and have incredibly fun times together.

When Rebekah first joined our family it so happened that none of us had a birthday between her arrival and her birthday. She didn't have a concept of what a birthday meant or what a party involved. We decided to keep things very simple for her. I explained to her that we would give her a box, and that when she opened it she would find something she really liked in the box. Then I asked her what she would like to find there.

"An apple?" she said. "Could I have an apple?"

"Oh, yes, honey. Apples are good. But for your birthday you can have something even more special than an apple. What would you like to find?" I said.

"Oh, Mommy, would you give me a watermelon?" she asked with delight.

And so for her sixth birthday—her first birthday in our family—Rebekah received an apple, a watermelon, and a bicycle.

BEING ON DISPLAY

Some adoptive families are not particularly noticeable. Perhaps the adopted children look very much like the parents and join the family in infancy. But for many adoptive families, any hope of leading a quiet, private life is over the moment they bring home an older child, a child of a different race, or a child with a physical, mental or emotional challenge.

Many of us enjoy watching people and trying to sort out their relationships, even though it's really none of our business. At a grocery store or restaurant we might find ourselves pondering if the fiftyish woman we see with a three year old is the child's mother or grandmother. If they are obviously of different ethnic groups we might wonder if the child is adopted or if the child's absent father provided the skin and hair color.

I think that recognizing that most of us do this sizing up of other families helps us understand why people are so curious about our own families. People enjoy sorting out relationships, and many people are very intrigued by the concept of adoption.

A few days ago I was at the orthodontist's office with Rebekah. I had Dinah with me, and one of the other waiting moms commented that she had considered adoption but had no idea how to get started. I was able to give her my name and phone number and look forward to answering her questions.

Sometimes when we're out in public we feel like we're ready to educate the world. We welcome questions and have business cards from our adoption ministry to give people and are wonderful advocates for adoption. Other times, though, we just want to enjoy time with our family and not be interrupted by others. At these times we focus on our kids and even avoid making eye contact with other people, thus discouraging conversation.

One night we took the whole family to The Spaghetti Factory for a special dinner. With eight children we don't have the resources to eat out very often, so it was a special treat. Our waitress, a sparkly nineteen year old, was quite interested in our family. After taking everyone's orders, she sweetly said to me, "Which of these children are yours?"

I responded, "They all are!"

She smiled at me and said, "But you know what I mean!"

I smiled back and said, "And you know what I mean!" which pretty much ended the conversation.

I feel it's most important when responding to peoples' comments and questions to affirm our listening children. I don't like to divide my children in people's minds into our "real" kids and our "adopted" kids, so I try not to discuss this with casual observers. I want my listening children to know that I consider all of them equally my "real" kids.

It can be somewhat disconcerting to know that people are watching your family and evaluating your children's behavior. It's easy to be tempted to want your kids to impress those watching. But ultimately it's more important for your child to feel secure in his place in your family and supported by you regardless of his behavior. Your goal is a strong relationship with your child, not a one-time chat with bystanders.

RACIAL ISSUES

If you adopt a child of a different race than yours, you need to be prepared not only to be on display but to hear comments, both intentional and unintentional, that may surprise you.

When Dinah had been in our family just a short time the receptionist at a medical appointment asked me her ethnicity. I replied, "Ethiopian."

The receptionist said, "So, African-American?"

Me: "Not really. Her ancestors haven't been in America for a few hundred years."

Receptionist: "Well I don't think every African country is in the computer!"

Me: "What do you put in the computer for someone from Russia? Do you put European or Russian?"

Receptionist: "Russian, of course!"

Me: "What about someone from Italy?"

Receptionist: "Italian. We have to because people from different countries in Europe are so different!"

Me: "I think you'd find that people from different countries in Africa are quite different as well."

Receptionist: "Oh, look! The computer does have Ethiopia listed! But I think it's the only African country in here. Let's look. Oh, the Marshall Islands are listed as well!"

Hmmm, last time I checked the Marshall Islands were in the Pacific Ocean. I don't think this woman meant to be unkind at all. Many people really do seem to think that Africa is one great big dark continent and that all Africans are basically the same. Many people think the same of Asians. The rich culture, history and geography of the various countries isn't commonly known. So don't be surprised at the things people say based on ignorance. We may not have known a lot about these countries, either, before we adopted our children.

Some parts of our country have very diverse populations, and other parts are very largely Caucasian. There will always be people who believe that races should remain separated and who don't appreciate you bringing a child of a race with which they don't feel comfortable into your home.

Children may make offensive comments. Unfortunately they are likely repeating things they have heard at home, and a little bit of reeducation from you can be very appropriate.

You may even hear comments that surprise you from people of your child's ethnic group. John is from an indigenous people group in India and his skin is very dark. Had he remained there he would be a Dalit, or untouchable. Though I don't see what difference this could possibly make in his new life in America, several times I have proudly introduced John to East Indians here and had them snub him and refuse to speak with him. Although the caste system is technically outlawed in India it obviously is still in effect.

As Christians we are to show acceptance and love for all people. We can model this for those around us as we become an unconsciously multi-racial family. Galatians 3:28 reminds us, "There is neither Jew nor Greek, there is neither slave nor free man, there is neither male nor female; for you are all one in Christ Jesus."

When people make foolish statements, such as asking if a Chinese child adopted as a baby will speak Chinese or English, we can answer with kindness rather than exasperation. The Lord can use our family to broaden people's views of the world. We don't want to ruin opportunities we have by responding rudely or with superiority.

Aaron will begin his freshman year at a state university in the fall. He was admitted to the freshman honors program, and I attended the orientation with him a few weeks ago. When we met with his advisor he mentioned that one of the things the committee had liked about Aaron was the fact that he had lived overseas for many years and that he came from a very diverse family.

He continued to explain that the students in the honors program would have the opportunity to travel to Rome during spring vacation. For most of the students, he said, it would be their first trip out of the United States.

I was quite troubled to think that the best and brightest young people at this university were approaching their university studies without ever having seen anything besides our very affluent, self-serving lifestyles in America. In fact, as we discussed fees for room and board I learned that the amount Aaron will pay for one quarter's meal tickets is roughly the same as I spend to feed our family of ten for two months. The students can use their meal tickets at several different dining halls, cafeterias and restaurants, resulting in the high cost.

Having indulged our young people their entire lives and trying to make their college experience as comfortable as possible, is it any wonder that they feel uncomfortable around people who seem different? When most sheltered Americans meet our racially diverse families they simply don't know what to think. It's outside their comfort zone.

Life can be uncomfortable for our children as well. Often they don't know where they fit in. A black child who has been raised in a white family, for example, doesn't really fit into the black community and may not feel accepted in the white community when she isn't with her family.

Sometimes adopted children feel like they don't really have any place where they fit in. They feel different in their own family, and they feel different among people of their racial heritage. Many adoption agencies now provide culture camps during which children can meet other adopted children of the same racial heritage, and it is among this group that some children feel the most comfortable. Other adopted children don't seem to struggle with racial issues very much. Each family needs to be sensitive to its own child.

The first time we took Dinah to visit some Caucasian friends who have three adopted African-American sons, their seven year old son Noah delightedly said, "Oh now, this is a girl I could marry!" He knew several black boys but no black girls, and apparently couldn't imagine an interracial marriage. As parents we need to explore our own feelings and see how comfortable we are with interracial dating and marriage, and help our children determine what they are comfortable with as well.

Perhaps quietly living our lives as multi-racial families and allowing the world to observe our healthy interactions will begin to eliminate some of the misconceptions people have.

CHAPTER THIRTEEN

Issues Affecting Different Ages

Some adoption issues vary depending on the age of your child when you adopt him.

BABIES

Bonding

Adopting a baby can be a very exciting experience. The fun of having a little one in your home is a daily adventure. There are a few things that can help make the experience easier.

There are differences, of course, between bringing a newborn home from the hospital and adopting a child who has spent a few months in foster care or an orphanage. Most of the issues discussed here relate to the child who is at least a few months old when she joins your family.

One of the first things you will do is take your baby for a thorough examination by your pediatrician. You will want to discuss issues appropriate to your child's age, of course, but you will most likely also have questions related to adoption. Your pediatrician may not understand how adoption issues affect her normal advice to families.

Dinah was nine months old when she arrived in our home. She was used to having a bottle of sweetened milk propped up in her crib around the clock. She had not been given solids. It was very difficult for her to sleep without a bottle. I tried giving her several types of pacifiers, but she refused to use them. I knew that it isn't a good idea to let babies sleep with bottles due to possible ear infections and dental problems.

When I told our pediatrician my concern about Dinah's sleep, he said she was much too old to need a bottle during the night and that I should simply let her cry. He said that it wasn't good for her to drink so much milk and that she needed to eat primarily solids.

I thought about this after leaving his office, and realized that I was more concerned about Dinah learning to trust me than I was about getting a good night's sleep. I decided that I would get up with her when she cried and feed her a diluted bottle of formula to begin to cut down on the amount of milk she was consuming. I would hold her while she drank her bottle and then return her to bed. If she continued to cry I would pat her and try to calm her to sleep.

This worked well and eventually I began to give Dinah a bottle of water rather than a milk bottle. Realizing that she seemed to need to suck throughout the night, I allowed her to take the water bottle to bed, knowing that it wouldn't have the same harmful effects as a milk bottle.

You will deal with different issues than we did, but my point is that you can't simply follow the pediatrician's advice. Helping Dinah learn to trust us was far more important than either her milk intake or potential ear infections.

It's very important to remember that we are living in a very fat, rich land with excellent medical care and very accessible prenatal care. Our babies grow differently here. Nutrition tends to be so good that babies are larger even at birth here than in many countries. Even our growth charts are different from many other countries. So if you adopt a baby internationally or from an impoverished background domestically you can't fairly compare that child with children who have had excellent nutrition all along.

Equally important is that you are your child's parent and will soon have a good feel for what is right for your child. Don't let anyone pressure you that you must follow our American time lines for raising your baby. My friend Terri 's adopted son, Elijah, was addicted to heroin at birth. She felt pressured into thinking that she had to wean Elijah on the same schedule that she had weaned her other babies. However, he desperately needed to suck for comfort. At less than eleven months he was completely weaned and even now, at age five, he has a deep need to chew and suck. He has had a terrible time with finger sucking and chewing on toys,. Terri believes that her desire to please people around her left him with some difficulties he is having a hard time overcoming. We strongly urge you to follow the time line that seems right for your baby.

There really is no rush to have our babies grow up sooner than they need to.

One of the most important things you can do to help your baby bond with you is to keep her with you constantly. She needs to have one primary caregiver, or have the job shared between her parents. Opinions vary as to how long you need to be the exclusive caregivers, and perhaps the optimum time varies from baby to baby. We began to see Dinah preferring me, with Steve as a second choice, very quickly. From her second day with us she began to reach for me if one of her siblings picked her up. Very quickly she began to smile delightedly when I would enter the room. She obviously was learning to trust me. We felt this was a very good sign.

Because we have many teenage children who enjoy helping with Dinah, we set some guidelines to give them an opportunity to participate in her care but to encourage her to continue to bond most strongly with me.

Dinah has been in our family nearly three months. At this point I am always the one to get up with her in the night, and I always go to her in the morning. I put her in her crib at night and pray with her before I leave the room. I usually feed her, and I bathe her each evening.

The children play with her throughout the day and occasionally feed and change her. It has worked very well for us. Dinah has her favorites among the children, as evidenced by her giggles when they approach. She responds well to all of them, but always prefers me when she is tired or hungry. Steve's role with her has primarily been that of a playmate, and she enjoys responding to him. Our one disappointment has been that Dinah doesn't enjoy being rocked or cuddled. She is a very active child and doesn't like to be still. Steve has taught her to hug, and she snuggles into his neck and lies quietly for a short time.

Development

Another area of concern you may have is your baby's development. Quite likely he will be behind his peers in his gross and fine motor skills and perhaps verbal skills as well. Many parents are concerned when they first meet their nine month old baby and find he can't roll over, or their thirteen month old baby and find she can't crawl.

Remember that most of these children have received very little individual attention and stimulation. Orphanage children typically spend most of their time lying on their back in a crib. Once they have a chance to be on the floor, with eager parents playing with them, many babies learn quickly. It's like watching a baby development film on fast forward, and so much fun!

If your baby doesn't seem to catch up quickly don't hesitate to discuss this with your pediatrician. There are early intervention programs that can help your child make up for lost time. Many of these programs are for children aged birth to three years old, so don't wait too long before inquiring about this for your child.

Food Issues

In the States most babies are started on solid foods when they are about four months old. If you adopted your baby internationally she may not have had any solids or may have been given cereal in her bottle. It's unlikely anyone would have had time to feed her with a spoon.

It takes some older babies awhile to adjust to the textures and tastes of solid foods. Some babies very much enjoy being offered solids.

Dinah never liked the texture or flavor of baby cereal, so after a few tries we gave up on it and began giving her oatmeal and Cream of Wheat instead. This she liked much better.

You may end up feeding your baby a bottle longer than pediatricians in the States normally recommend. If that is how your baby feels comforted and if it helps him feel safe in his rather scary new world, what harm can a few extra months with a bottle do?

Routines

Many families like to get their baby on a routine—naps at approximately the same time each day, feeding at approximately the same times—and this helps everyone's life flow so much easier.

It may take awhile to get your new baby to adjust to the routine you'd like. Some babies seem to struggle for a few weeks with the time difference and jet lag they experienced traveling to the States. Some babies like to sleep a lot, almost as if they are avoiding all the stimulation of their new life, and others are very wakeful, wanting to constantly interact with people.

Try to get a feel for your baby's preferences and moods. If something seems too unusual don't hesitate to consult your pediatrician.

We really had no intention of adopting a nine month old baby. In fact, even just a few weeks before I traveled to Ethiopia to bring Andrew and Dinah home, Steve and I discussed the possibility of just adopting Andrew. With our oldest child twenty years old and our youngest child nine, it seemed so silly to consider a baby.

But obviously the Lord knew exactly what our family needed. We are having the time of our lives enjoying this little girl. Our older children vie to feed and change her, and I sometimes wonder if she will have the chance to learn how to entertain herself. Whenever she is peacefully playing in the living room one of the children inevitably walks through, says, "Dinah, you are so sweet!" and picks her up. They all enjoy playing with her and she is a very good natured baby. But why shouldn't she be, with nine older family members doting on her?

We've decided every family needs a baby! A little one gives everyone a good excuse to be silly and to slow down the pace of life. Although we don't have quite the energy we did when our older children were babies, we find that we are more relaxed with this little one.

TODDLERS

Adopting a child between eighteen and thirty-six months of age may be the most challenging of all adoptions. These little ones have hopefully bonded with their caregivers, whether that is a foster mother, birth mother, or orphanage worker, and feel a tremendous loss when they leave their familiar environment.

In addition, they are too young to understand why they are leaving. When children are four or older someone can explain to them that they are going to have a new family. The child won't understand all that is involved, but at least can participate in good-byes. To a toddler, the whole experience is usually very overwhelming and he may seem very sad for some time.

If you adopt a toddler, many families have found that it is helpful to make a gradual transition between caregivers. If you can meet your child and spend time with her over several days, without completely taking her away from her familiar caregiver, it can help her transition be easier. She can learn to feel comfortable with you without at the same time dealing with feelings of loss.

Once your toddler is home you should be prepared for his behavior to revert to that of a younger child. Often toddlers who, according to regular development charts should no longer drink bottles, enjoy being rocked and fed like younger children. It helps them feel secure and begin to trust you. Making eye contact while giving your toddler a bottle, rocking and singing to her can be a special time for both of you.

As with infants, it is important for bonding with your toddler that you stay with her around the clock for several weeks as much as possible. She needs to learn that you are a constant in her life and that in the midst of change and loss she can count on you.

Realize that children of any age who have spent time in an orphanage may have self-stimulating behaviors. Because they may not have received much attention these children developed habits to comfort themselves. Sometimes this might involve head-banging or staring at their hands. For several years Deborah rocked herself to sleep at night, rocking from side to side, sometimes quite rapidly, which shook the bed. She would do this even if we rocked her before putting her to bed. It was a long-ingrained habit and made us sad, feeling like we weren't meeting all her needs. Even now, after seven years in our home, she occasionally rocks when very tired or stressed.

Recognizing that these behaviors are a way your child comforts himself may help you to deal with them.

SCHOOL AGE CHILDREN

Adopting a school age child can be a lot of fun. It can also be highly stressful if you aren't prepared for the issues with which you are likely to be confronted.

I have addressed many of these issues throughout this book, so I'll just mention a few more suggestions that have proven helpful for many families.

Find a Strength

It is helpful to find something at which your child can be successful. Children adopted at an older age have missed out on many common childhood experiences and normally lag behind their age mates not only academically but in other ways as well. They have typically not had the opportunity to play organized sports, take music lessons, raise a pet or learn 4-H skills.

If you discover something at which your child is successful, you may want to enable your child to become even more skilled in that area. When a child knows he does well at something, it doesn't seem to matter as much that he struggles in other areas.

Rebekah has always struggled academically, but we found that she is quite good at gymnastics and for several years we fit her club fees into our tight budget so that she could continue to improve in this area. It boost her self-confidence and gave her a very fun activity to which she could look forward.

After a few years Rebekah's skills developed to the point that she was asked to join her club's team and begin to compete with other clubs. Our family had to do some serious thinking about this. In talking with other families we learned that when a child is on a gymnastics team it is a major commitment for the family, both financially and time-wise. We had to decide if we wanted our family's weekends to largely be spent traveling to Rebekah's gymnastics meets. Eventually we decided that, though we were glad Bek had enjoyed gymnastics and done so well, it was time for her to move on to other activities. Still, she will be able to participate on the high school gymnastics team in another year, and that will be a way for her to find her niche in school.

Through the elementary school track program John discovered that not only does he love to run, but he is quite good as well. The first year he was eligible to participate in track the coaches made certain that, because of his extremely limited vision, he always ran in lane one. At meet after meet he won his races against children with normal vision. The next year the coaches didn't make any special concessions for John and he still won. This has become an enjoyable activity for John and been a wonderful opportunity for him to compete with his sighted classmates.

Affection

Don't expect the child you adopted at an older age to immediately be affectionate verbally or physically. Although you have the title and role of mom or dad, your child doesn't know you and really has no reason to be affectionate. I have had people express shock when hearing this, saying, "But aren't the children grateful that you adopted them?" If you think about it, why should they be? You've taken your child away from everything familiar to him—his language, his friends, his familiar sights and smells—and brought him to what seems like a different planet. Yes, you've given him the opportunity for a better life in many ways, but he likely grieves for the things he lost as well.

It can be a hard time for children. They know they should be grateful—they were probably told by their former caregivers that they should behave themselves and appreciate all they have available now—but they might feel pretty homesick, too.

If they feel pressure from their new parents to show affection before they're ready it can be quite stressful and insincere. It's much better to give your child time to feel genuine emotions than to cause her to feel that she should manufacture feelings too soon.

157

Each morning after Andrew joined our family I would pray with John, Deborah and him at the door, hug each child, say I loved him or her and wish them a good day. John and Deborah would hug me back and say they loved me. Andrew would say something like, "Bye, Mom! Have good day!"

We followed this pattern for several weeks, and when the children were home from school we talked and did school work and played and prayed. Mid-way through the last week of school, after I gave each child my little speech, Andrew turned, gave me a big hug, said, "I love you, Mom!" and headed out the door. I was surprised but delighted.

That night when I tucked the boys into bed Andrew threw his arms around me, hugged me very tightly, kissed me several times, and again said "I love you." Whether or not Andrew actually loves me at this point I'm not sure, but I'm pleased that he feels comfortable enough to be demonstrative and that he seems to understand that we have a special relationship.

There is no way to predict how long it will take for your child to feel comfortable showing you affection. Some children are never physically demonstrative. Others may be affectionate immediately, but without a lot of meaning behind it. Do what feels comfortable to you, but don't require your child to say or do anything that makes him feel uncomfortable in this area. Especially if you have other children, your new child will see how you interact and may want to be part of it. If not, you can love your child more than you thought imaginable without receiving a physical response back.

Sometimes it might seem like your child is on the outside looking in. She observes your family and seems to want to be part of it, but doesn't join in and participate. I often feel that John is this way. He watches the rest of us but doesn't join in our conversations unless we ask him specific questions. When we visit my parents, a five hour drive, he prefers to ride the entire trip without talking. We have to make an effort to draw him into our conversation or games.

Does it seem too risky to participate, or is being quiet and staying out of the way so habitual for him? We are uncertain, but want him to know he is a valued family member. We ask his opinion and do all we can to include him. This area has improved a bit in the three years John has been in our family. We also recognize that helping a child feel he belongs involves both effort on our part and a willingness to try on his part.

Acting Younger Than Their Age

Our older adopted children often missed out on much of the nurturing we give to babies and preschoolers. Sometimes it's helpful if we try to fill in some of these gaps for them. Tonight I rocked Dinah as I fed her a bottle. As we rocked I sang her a little song I'd altered for her. Deborah watched from across the room and asked if I would rock her after I put Dinah to bed.

Soon I was rocking my lovely eleven year old daughter, singing her a special song we used to sing years ago. She sang along and smile happily.

I noticed Andrew watching us and chuckling, so when we were finished I asked him if he would like me to rock him. He said yes, and soon was on my lap, though not sitting in a very cuddly position. I rocked him and sang to him, a special song about being glad that God gave him to our family. When we finished I rubbed his soft head and told him I am very glad God let us have him in our family. He hugged me harder than he ever had and said, "I too, Mommy, I glad too!"

These special times of filling in some of these missing gaps for our children can go a long way to building strong bonds between us.

Their Missing History

A major challenge when adopting older children, either internationally or domestically, is that they have years of history about which we know nothing. We can never go back and learn about all that happened to them in their first years of life. Even when their English improves and they tell us stories of their early life they won't tell us everything. Some things they don't remember, and other things they just don't consider important enough to share. Additionally, their perception of an event may not have been accurate, so what they do tell us may or may not have happened the way they describe.

It's sad to realize our child has undergone many things that we'll never know about, things that shaped our child into the person he is today. We need to start building memories today.

When your child does share with you something that happened in the years before she was in your home, it's a good idea to write the story down. You want to remember details, names and chronology that your child may forget. You will provide your child with a very special gift if you keep these memories for her. You'll enjoy reading the stories over and over also. Eventually you may gain enough information from your child that you can put stories in order and have a clearer perspective of your child's early years.

Remember that your child needs time to learn your family's habits, routines and personalities. Don't expect too much too fast. Perhaps you can remember when you were getting to know your spouse. In most cases the relationship took time to develop, sometimes several years. Give this new relationship the benefit of time as well.

CHAPTER FOURTEEN

Keeping Your Child's Cultural Heritage

by Peter Gardner

A bonus of adopting children internationally or from a different background domestically is that your family can enjoy many different cultural experiences. This can be a very rewarding aspect of adoption. It might seem as if the easiest, most effective thing to do would be to immerse the child in Americana. This way, it might be thought, the new child will become more quickly Americanized. I would caution against this, however. You would be doing your child, as well as your entire family, a grave disservice.

Instead of discouraging these different cultural patterns from entering your family, support them. For example, we celebrate Chinese New Year in honor of Rebekah from China. We have a collection of various objects from the adopted children's respective countries: matryoshka dolls from Russia, wooden elephants from India, and an entire menagerie of animals from Ethiopia. We prominently display these in our house, encouraging questions that they raise. We treat each question that arises as an opportunity to share our love of different cultures with others.

And because we have this affection for these different countries, it provides the kids a connection with their birth land. We want them not only to love their birth land, but the people who still live there. We hope that someday they might desire to have an influence on these people. Rebekah has already expressed a desire to go to China as a missionary, something that would be easy for her to do, having lived there before, and having a connection to the people of that country. It would be much easier for her to enter China than for us to do so as Caucasians.

My sister Dinah is incredibly cute. It's interesting to us that she seems to be very attracted to other brown people. When brown people talk with her or hold her, she has a very sweet habit of gently placing her hands on the sides of their faces and staring into their eyes. She doesn't do this with white people. It's as though it brings back a memory to her of her early days. There aren't a lot of brown people in Spokane, but we are enjoying the opportunity to make new friends and expand our understanding.

My brothers and sisters enjoy going to restaurants that serve food from their birth countries. It's not just the food that they enjoy, but the whole atmosphere. They like the music, the décor, the smells and the other patrons. We always get a kick out of their delight in these experiences. Our whole family has developed a taste for food from all of the different countries represented in our home. We enjoy eating Ethiopian injera with our hands and using chopsticks to eat Chinese food. In fact, we have made a tradition of going out for Chinese food every Christmas eve.

We try to learn a little bit of each of the kids' first language. Even though the kids tend to forget their first language pretty quickly, we still incorporate a few phrases into our family life. We always learn how to say "I love you" in our brothers' and sisters' languages and say it to them at bedtime or when they seem sad.

It's a responsibility to be the older sibling of adopted kids, but I know I've gained a lot from it. We all have a lot of respect for other cultures. When I graduate from college in two years I plan to be involved in some type of missions work overseas. At the moment I am considering working on a ship such as Logos II or Doulos. This work involves living and working with people from over forty countries. I don't know if I would feel comfortable doing this if I hadn't already learned to appreciate other cultures through my siblings.

CHAPTER FIFTEEN

Sibling Issues

by Aaron Gardner

I sit here writing this while my family enjoys our vacation at Nine Mile Resort outside of Spokane. Mom is going over a final draft of her book, Dad is headed back to the city in search of an "O-ring" for our camping stove, Peter is back in Spokane at work, and the other kids are performing various activities. Deborah and Andrew are searching for tadpoles and fish with some newly found friends, Susannah is gazing into the falling sun, Rebekah is assisting Dinah in floundering about the tranquil lake, and John—*where is John?*

After a brief yet somewhat frenetic search, I find that John has gone after the stove part with my dad, and my mind returns to its peaceful focus. But this typifies the Gardner family life. It is difficult, nigh impossible, to keep track of the young people who roam my home.

And I wouldn't change a thing. The frustrations and angst associated with an eight sibling family can be daunting at the least, but with each addition another unique element is added to the mix. John, the peaceful introvert; Rebekah, an animated moderate; Deborah, the outspoken livewire; Andrew, the vivacious and lovable pest. These constituents provide not only occasional difficulties, but also a serene balance to all of our lives.

Amidst the trials and tranquility, it is easy to go through the day perceiving everyone, but not really connecting with them. It is tough to maintain a relationship with a parent while seven other children require their attention. That is why I am pleased that my parents have taken chances to build real relationships away from home life. Throughout the years, my dad and I have risen early on Friday mornings to go out to breakfast at Shari's. This has given us a chance to study various books we read by great Christian authors, to talk about school, plans for the future, girls, home life, and to just bond together apart from everyone else. My mom also takes Susannah or Rebekah out for tea once a week, and in this way they experience this relationship as well. Because of this trust built through the years, I would never hesitate to ask for parental advice on any subject.

This next fall starts a fresh chapter in my life as I leave to attend school at Eastern Washington University. I've had my share of rough times at home, but I still know I'm going to miss it. My brothers and sisters and my parents have meant so much to me, teaching me how to relate to people with a wide variety of characteristics, instructing me in patience, persistence, faith, and love. I am so thankful that each of them has been with me throughout the years, to help turn me into the man I am today.

PART THREE

Looking at the Future

CHAPTER SIXTEEN

If the Dream Becomes a Nightmare

For most of you this chapter is unnecessary. Perhaps you got off to a bumpy start with your child, but several months have passed, you've all gotten to know each other and life is nearly back to normal, only better. But some of you are crying out for someone to understand the heartache you're feeling.

Your child is home, you've given all of you several months to adjust, and you honestly feel like this is worse than the worst nightmare you could have imagined. Do you just have to endure the rest of your life, barely making it through each miserable day? Is there any hope that life will be full of joy again?

I'm going to share with you a very painful time in our family's life to give a foundation to this issue. In order to protect the privacy of the child involved I've changed his name and other identifying details.

After John had been in our home awhile, but before we adopted Andrew and Dinah, we decided to see about bringing a long-term foster care child into our home. Many people had questioned our international adoptions and asked us why we hadn't adopted domestically. It was a good question, and we decided to pursue welcoming a hard-to-place child, probably with serious medical issues, into the family. We began to work with a private agency that typically placed children in long-term foster care situations. The children weren't necessarily legally free, but weren't expected to be returned to their parents, either.

The private agency was contracted to find homes for children who were wards of the state but for whom the state was having difficulty finding families. We were attracted to this program because each social worker had just a few cases so we felt we would be able to access the support we needed, and we would very likely be able to keep the child in our home until he or she graduated from high school.

After we completed all the necessary training months passed without a child being offered to us. As we look back we understand that the agency was facing some challenges and that the state wasn't contacting them about available children regularly, but we didn't know that at the time. We knew there were hundreds of children needing families in our state, so it seemed odd that we weren't being called.

We called the agency regularly and asked about possible children. Finally they told us about a twelve year old boy who might be a possibility. Although he didn't have severe medical issues, he had a low I.Q. and serious behavioral problems. We would be his eleventh placement, and his last several placements had been in group homes rather than in families. As the caseworker read us information on Burt, we were intrigued and agreed to a meeting.

Our first meeting went so much better than we had expected. We took just Susannah with us so that we wouldn't overwhelm Burt with the whole family. He asked if we liked to play games and brought out a Monopoly set. We spent an hour playing and chatting, and although he didn't really follow the rules he did better than we had thought he would.

Several additional visits followed, with Burt eventually spending a weekend in our home. The first time he met Deborah he asked if he could help her put her socks on, which was a very encouraging sign to us. We had been concerned that he might express discomfort with her physical abnormalities. He enjoyed playing with the children and followed our instructions well. We wondered what everyone was so worried about. Things seemed to be going incredibly well.

Eventually everyone agreed that this might work and Burt moved into our home. For a few days things went well. Then we began to see lying, intentional destruction of property, feces smeared in his room, severe anger and physical aggression toward our other children. Suddenly watching Burt became our full time occupation. Steve and I never let him out of our sight, and that caused a host of additional problems. He was angry that the other children could play in the backyard and he couldn't unless I had time to go outside with him. The other children could go across the street to play in the park, but he couldn't because, as a foster child, he had to be with someone who was licensed to care for him.

He constantly begged us to adopt him so that he could have more freedom. We explained to him that he had to show us he could handle freedom. Things got worse and worse.

Eventually he became extremely defiant and refused to do what I asked him to do. If I needed him to get in the car so that I could pick one of the other children up from an activity he refused to get in. There was very little I could do. I would tell him he would lose a privilege, but being in control mattered more to him than having a treat later. He seemed to enjoy power struggles, and much as I tried to avoid them it was impossible because, in order to keep our family running smoothly, there were certain things I needed to do and places I needed to go, and I needed him to accompany me. He was bigger than me, and that increased my feeling of powerlessness as I wondered if he might use physical force against me. And of course according to foster care rules I couldn't touch him, and he knew I couldn't force him to do anything.

Steve, Burt and I began going for weekly counseling to a woman with a lot of expertise in attachment issues. When she read Burt's paperwork she said he was perhaps the most hurt child she had ever dealt with. Although this overwhelmed us, it also made us more determined than ever that we wanted to make this placement work. We didn't want to be one more disappointment in his life. The counseling was discouraging, though. The counselor told me that I couldn't parent Burt the same way I parented our other children. She said that I relied on a reciprocal relationship of love and respect with my children, and I couldn't do that with Burt. I needed to be totally non-emotional and non-feeling in my relationship with him, and deal with logical consequences.

I soon realized that I couldn't parent six children one way and one child another way, especially when two or more of the children had been involved in the same situation. If Burt and Deborah had a confrontation, for example, I struggled with dealing with Deborah in one way and Burt in another way. It was very difficult for all of us.

In the midst of all of this, Burt enjoyed going to church with us very much. People there told us what a wonderful job we were doing with him. His ready grin won him quite a following. No one had any idea of what went on at home, and we weren't free to share our struggles even with our closest friends.

The defiance accelerated into abusive language, primarily directed toward me, and a total lack of cooperation. I began to feel trapped in my own home.

Steve and I spent many nights wondering what had happened to our family and how we could honor the Lord in this. We felt we were ignoring our other children because of the need to spend hours each day dealing with Burt. We struggled and prayed over what to do. My heart broke at the thought of failing Burt. We also felt strongly that we were beginning to fail our other children. We had nothing left to give any of them and nothing left to give each other.

Then one horrifying night Burt crept into one of our daughter's rooms while she was asleep. Thankfully we found him very soon. This was our line in the sand, the line we couldn't allow to be crossed. We realized that, regardless of how much we wanted this to work, we couldn't risk the safety of our other children.

A few days later Burt was removed from our home. The director of his new group home came to pick him up, and he left without a backward glance. I was in tears as they drove away, wondering how something that had seemed so right could end up so terribly wrong.

In retrospect we feel like this placement was doomed to failure from the beginning. Although we had successfully adopted older children, our experience with children with physical disabilities had not prepared us to parent a child with serious emotional and behavioral challenges. Burt hated having a different last name and different rules than our other children, and his status as a foster child in a family of adopted children was a continual frustration to him. He struggled daily with trying to decide whether he really wanted to belong to a family or not. Family life requires a certain amount of cooperation not needed in a group home setting.

I wish that we had talked with families with a combination of birth children and adopted children who were successfully parenting foster children as well. We should have talked with families who took on the challenge of a severely behaviorally challenged child and gotten their input as to how they made it work. Having this knowledge in advance may have helped us see that such a placement most likely wouldn't work for us at this time in our lives. Had we still accepted the placement the support system may have given us the necessary help we needed.

For weeks I grieved the failure of this placement. For some reason it hit me the hardest at church. Each week as I listened to the sermon I felt weepy and lost. Steve and I wondered if I would ever feel healed. The rest of the family felt incredible relief to have their home back to normal, but I couldn't stop wishing we could have helped this child.

We believe that Burt may have been successful had he been placed with empty nesters who could devote the majority of their time to him, or in a family with only much older teenagers. With several of our children very close in age to Burt it created a safety issue for them and a great deal of competition for everyone. We understand these issues now but weren't aware of them when we accepted the placement.

I believe that I really didn't heal until we decided to adopt again and made a commitment to Andrew and Tsahaynesh. I believe the Lord gave us the opportunity, through welcoming other children into our home, to be reminded that we could continue to make a difference for needy children.

Your story is probably quite different than ours. You may be struggling over completely different issues. But the feeling of loss and failure may be the same.

In a Leadership Summit our church recently hosted Andy Stanley shared that we might have the right vision, but be using the wrong strategy. (1) Because things aren't working out doesn't mean the Lord didn't call you to adopt. Your vision and understanding of His call may be right on course. But you might be using a strategy that isn't most effective. We discovered that we do well with older physically challenged children, but are probably not able, at this point in our lives, to be successful with children with serious emotional and behavioral issues. That doesn't mean we can't effectively do what the Lord has asked us to do.

An important concept in the adoption world is that of a "family fit." Nancy Spoolstra, who has done a great deal of work with attachment issues, explains that typically parents want reciprocal relationships with their children. There is an anticipation that the children will give as well as receive, become interactive in developing an existing family ethos, and that parents will be enriched by their adoptive children as much as they enrich their children. (2)

Doris Landry, who also works in the area of attachment, states that there is no prospective parent who could envisage the reality of some of the problems a hurt child brings to an adoptive relationship. She insists parenting any special needs child is a special and huge undertaking; it may challenge a family for life. The issues are parallel for birth-families and adoptive families . . . the element of surprise at issues can stun in both. (3)

In her website, www.radzebra.org, Nancy Spoolstra claims that many families, whether adopting internationally or domestically, are expecting to adopt a cute little Shetland pony, but instead find themselves living with an undomesticated zebra! They look so much like horses, but when you live with one for awhile you realize that this child is not the same breed as the others. Although the zebra can be domesticated, it will always be a zebra—the first to startle and the last to relax when faced with stress or danger. (4)

Perhaps you were expecting a pony and got a zebra. What do you do now? EMK Press has an excellent article available on-line at *www.emkpress.com* entitled "Disruption and Dissolution: Unspoken Losses," edited by Sheena Macrae. This article is a good starting point in helping you understand what can go wrong and what perhaps can be done to help. It includes a helpful list of additional resources.

The caveat is that none of this research and help addresses the problem from a Christian perspective. And I believe that our confidence in the Lord's direction and His ability to give us the strength we need each day truly should be a factor in our perspective on raising difficult children. However, I well know from my experience with Burt that prayer and faith alone are often not enough to enable us to successfully parent difficult children. We need to draw on every resource available.

It can be very hard to admit that you're struggling. Give yourself permission to acknowledge to yourself, the Lord, and others that you are having a difficult time. You don't need to blame yourself. You don't need to blame your child. You don't need to blame other family members. Many children whose adoptions are so stressful that they end up being disrupted go on to do well in another family. That doesn't mean there was something wrong with your family. You may simply not have the resources or training to meet the needs of this child.

But your heart may cry out that you felt so sure that parenting this child was what the Lord wanted you to do! How could you have been so wrong?

There are some things to consider before you do something drastic. First, how long has this child been in your home? Have you given all of you time to adjust? Do things seem to be getting slowly better, or are they getting worse? Does she simply have behaviors that frustrate and annoy you, or is your entire household in chaos and upheaval constantly?

Today I received a frantic email from a good friend who just returned from overseas with four year old and twenty-three month old sisters. The girls were living in separate foster homes so don't know each other. The parents' trip overseas was completed in four days. The younger girl's foster mother nearly refused to turn her over to her new parents and created extreme tension for the little girl. My friends are wondering if they can successfully parent these children. They are all extremely exhausted, the little one has cried almost non-stop and the stress level is high.

Unless this couple panics and makes a hasty, frantic decision, this adoption probably won't result in disruption. The parents will catch up on their sleep, the children will begin to settle in, and the family can help the little ones deal with the grief and loss they are experiencing. But right now the family feels like they didn't get the right message from the Lord.

If you feel this way, I urge you to get counseling from someone who understands not only adoption issues but attachment challenges as well. Go online and find a list-serv for people who have disrupted or are considering disrupting an adoption. Find respite care for your child. Look at the resources I mentioned above.

Another useful website is *www.drfederici.com*. Dr. Federici has developed techniques to help children whose families have tried everything else and failed. An experienced adoptive father, his insights and techniques are different than many others, but certainly worth investigating.

What is your line in the sand that you can't allow to be crossed? For us it was the safety of our other children. For you it will be something different. What would make this placement absolutely intolerable?

Can you put yourself in your child's shoes? What would it be like to suddenly be in a different environment, forever? Terri Bade remembers being dropped off at a cousin's house for a week's stay when she didn't really know that cousin and their home was quite different from what she was used to. The smells, the food, the bedroom, the playthings, and their lifestyle all were so different. The only familiar thing she had was herself. It was scary and very uncomfortable. She remembers pining for home, and that when her mother arrived to pick her up she raced to the car, never wanting to go back. But our adopted children never will see mom or anyone else from their past again. There is no "normal" to which they can run back. It helps if you can get a glimpse of the fear and insecurity our children feel.

Then, if you've done everything you know to do and things continue to get worse, perhaps the Lord intended to use you in this child's life in a different way than you had planned. Maybe your part was to provide a way for this child to be taken from poverty, abuse and neglect and brought to our very rich country where there are resources to help him. Maybe you were to provide a family for a child trapped in the foster care system so that she could move on to a successful permanent placement.

Remember our discussion in chapter three about the Law of Linearity? We tend to feel that if we are patient, use excellent parenting skills, read enough books, and take our child to church regularly God will reward us with a successful parent-child relationship. He might, or He might not. He sees the big picture, the end from the beginning, and also knows what He wants to teach us and how He wants to bring glory to Himself. As Larry Crabb reminds us, the pressure's off. "The arrangement under which the Better Life of Blessings is promised to those who perfectly follow God's principles has been replaced by a new arrangement. Now the Better Hope of Intimacy with a God who sovereignly assigns or withholds blessings according to an unseen plan is available. And it's available at every moment and in every circumstance to those who come to God on Jesus' coattails." (5)

That's very freeing. We can do all that we know to do, follow biblical principles, commit our way to the Lord, and then we can relax and trust that He is at work and the result will be due to His pleasure, not our efforts.

That might seem so unfair, but God is God. As John Piper reminds us, "We are creatures, and our Creator is not bound or obligated to give us anything—not life or health or anything. He gives, he takes, and he does no injustice (Job 1:21) . . . . Therefore every breath we take, every time our heart beats, every day the sun rises, every moment we see with our eyes or hear with our ears or speak with our mouths or walk with our legs is, for now, a free and undeserved gift to sinners who deserve only judgment." (6)

Beloved fellow traveler on this adoption journey, let's pray for our children and ourselves, seek counsel and support and wisdom from those who have walked this road before us, and ultimately recognize that the King of the Universe is in control of the end of our story. He is worthy of our trust.

Notes:

1. Willow Creek Leadership conference, Andy Stanley.
2. Sheena Macrae, *Disruption &Dissolution: Unspoken Losses* (*www.emkpress.com*), 2
3. Ibid., 2
4. Nancy Spoolstra, *www.radzebra.org*
5. Larry Crabb, *The Pressure's Off* (Colorado Springs, Colorado: Waterbrook Press, 2002), 33.
6. John Piper, *Don't Waste Your Life* (Wheaton, Illinois: Crossway Books, 2003), 51,52.

CHAPTER SEVENTEEN

Support Groups

$\mathscr{T}$alking with others who have gone or are going through the issues you're struggling with can be one of the best ways of dealing with adoption stress. Support groups can be invaluable. There may already be a support group in your area. If not, you might want to start one.

If you choose to form a support group, you will need to consider several things:

1. What is the purpose of your support group?

Do you want to raise awareness about adoption in general? Do you want to challenge your church to see adoption as a ministry? Perhaps you want to spend time praying for the needs of the adoptive and pre-adoptive families in your group. Do you want experienced adoptive families to provide support for families just getting started? Do you want adopted children to meet each other?

2. For whom is the group designed?

Groups can be for adoptive parents with or without including children. Groups can be specifically for families who have children of a certain age or have adopted from a specific country. Prospective adoptive parents can be included in the group. Will you just invite church families to your group, or will you advertise to the community? The purpose of your group will help determine the answer to this.

3. How often will the group meet?

Monthly or quarterly often works well. Some groups meet weekly, at least for a time. It can be difficult to sustain enthusiasm when meeting that frequently, but it may be appropriate in some situations.

4. Where will the group meet?

Options might include your church or homes of participating families. Some groups rotate between homes of group members. If children are included, be certain that there is room for them to play away from the adults if you will discuss things to which you don't necessarily want them to listen. It can be helpful if older children are available to watch younger ones so that the adults aren't interrupted. Be sure there are convenient restrooms.

5. What will the format of the meetings be?

You might have a topic for each meeting and invite guest speakers. You might let families share challenges with which they are dealing and spend time praying for each family and their situation. Consider whether your purpose is primarily educational or supporting individual families.

You can look in the yellow pages under "adoption" or "abortion alternatives" and find professionals who might be willing to talk with your group about relevant topics. Perhaps experienced adoptive families might be willing to share also. Do some checking on the potential speaker's experience and perspective on a topic before giving the go-ahead to speak.

6. How will you advertise the meetings?

Certainly you will advertise in your church bulletin and probably with posters in your church. Consider whether you want to invite families from other churches to participate. If so, you will need to contact the churches and ask them to advertise in their bulletin and with posters also. A phone call may be sufficient, but you might want to make an appointment with the senior pastor or adult ministries pastor to explain the purpose and value of the support group. You may also want to advertise on local Christian radio stations if they run complimentary Public Service Announcements.

Your group may have just a few regular attendees. Most likely people will come for awhile and then stop as their needs change. It can require a fair amount of effort on your part to keep the group running, but the support it can provide to families, especially in times of crisis, is well worth the effort. Spending time listening to families and praying about their concerns is one of the most supportive things you can do.

CHAPTER EIGHTEEN

Ready to Adopt Again?

For some of you, things may be going so well that you are considering adding another child or two to your family. When adoption works well it is possibly the most exciting, rewarding way you can spend your life. Seeing the progress the children make and growing more and more in love with each other is very fulfilling.

A week ago we heard that the African Children's Choir was going to be singing at a church near our home. We thought Andrew might enjoy it, so we took the family to hear the choir. Andrew's reaction was even better than we had hoped. He was fascinated and enjoyed each song. After awhile he climbed up on my lap, took my arms and wrapped them around himself, and leaned his head back on my shoulder. "Thank you, Mom!" he said. "Thank you so much you bring me." If that's not enough to make a tired mom feel like it's all worthwhile, I don't know what is.

Tonight as Susannah and I were cooking dinner little Dinah crawled into the kitchen and proceeded to entertain us with her repertoire of tricks. She made a fish face, blew kisses, and clapped and clapped until she made herself giddy with excitement and fun. She chuckled in her surprisingly deep voice and thoroughly distracted us from our work. What could be more fun?

So how do you decide if it's time to adopt again? There are a few questions you might want to consider.

First, how long has your child been in your home? Many adoption agencies require families to wait at least six months before starting another adoption, and I think it's a good rule. Even the very quickest adoptions usually take four to six months from the time the family starts the paperwork until their new child is home, so families are usually looking at a minimum of ten to twelve months between adoptions. Each child needs a chance to thoroughly adapt to his new family and this is probably the minimum time required. There are, of course, exceptions to this, but it's a good rule of thumb.

Second, what sort of adoption are you considering the second time around? Will you adopt from the same country from which you adopted the first time, or again through foster care or a domestic adoption? What age child are you considering? Do you want to adopt in birth order, or would you consider a child older than the child already in your home?

Third, how will you afford another adoption? If you are in debt from the first adoption it would be wise to pay those bills before incurring more. You might consider inviting friends, family and church members to have a part in providing a family for a child by encouraging them to participate in a fund-raising program such as the one available through Kingdom Kids Adoption Ministries. This program is described in the Appendix.

Fourth, are you and your spouse in agreement that it is time to consider adopting again? In many cases either the husband or wife is ready to go and the other person's enthusiasm is lagging behind. How will you work together as a couple to resolve this? How important is it to you that you be in agreement on this?

Fifth, how will adding another child to your family affect your family dynamics? If you have other children how have they adjusted to your first adopted child? Are they enthusiastic about adding another sibling to the family? Have you seen them grow and mature through the addition of your first adopted child? Are they still struggling? How much pressure can you put on them to step out of their comfort zone?

Sixth, although there are surely issues with which you are continuing to deal, do you have an overall feeling that things have gone well? Has your family life settled into some semblance of a routine and normalcy? On a day to day basis does life seem good? Adopting another child isn't going to solve unresolved problems.

Seventh, do you feel the Lord calling you to minister to another child? Does being an adoptive parent give you joy unlike anything else? Are you willing to take a risk, knowing that a second adoption may be much more difficult than the first adoption?

I urge you to discuss these questions with your spouse, spend time in prayer, and, if everything seems positive, joyfully step out in faith, asking the Lord to open and close doors as you plan to welcome another child into your family.

Some of you, perhaps a small percentage, will become passionate about adoption and not want to stop! You are the ones who end up with eight, twelve or fifteen children in your home and manage to make it all look easy.

So how do you know when it's time to adopt again, or even if you should consider adopting again? How do you know when your family is definitely complete?

I've been asking myself those questions quite a bit lately. I'm having a very personal struggle that may help you make some hard decisions yourself. When Susannah and I were in Ethiopia three months ago we spent several days at three different orphanages. The adoption agency we used makes a video every couple of months of the children who are waiting for families. When we visited one of the orphanages a five year old girl I had seen on several of the videos came running up to us with a huge smile. Susannah played games with the children, and this little girl caught on to them more easily than any of the other children. My brother-in-law, Dave, was wearing a shirt with words on it, and as he held Medrawit she pointed to each letter and said its name. She was a very charming little girl, quite unlike the way she came across on the videos.

Unfortunately, she has a herpes infection on her face which has been difficult to clear up. A doctor's opinion is that, once in the States, it will clear up completely. Whether or not it will recur remains to be seen.

Susannah and I were so taken with Medrawit that, when we visited the orphanage for older children, we made it a point to look for her seven year old sister, Samrawit. Unlike her bubbly, vivacious sister, Samrawit is quiet and shy but incredibly sweet. Her eyelids are droopy, giving her a sleepy appearance, but this can be surgically corrected fairly easily. Because we were paying quite a bit of attention to her she quietly said to me, "You my mommy?" I asked one of the older boys who speaks English well to explain to her that I wasn't her mommy, but that I would try to find a mommy for her.

A few days later we were back at the orphanage, talking with several of the children. I saw Samrawit out of the corner of my eye. She kept watching us, sizing us up, and then bravely came forward, took my hand, pulled my ear down to her level, and said, "Please you my mommy?"

Oh my! The things a child can do to a person's heart! Through tears I told her again that I would try to find a mommy for her.

And try I have. I have many contacts through my work with Kingdom Kids Adoption Ministries, and I have asked dozens of families if they would consider adding these sisters to their family. Perhaps because they don't come across well on the videos, or perhaps because of their medical issues, no one has expressed the slightest interest. We have set up a fund at Kingdom Kids to help with the cost of their adoption, and even this bait hasn't attracted anyone.

As I've contacted people an interesting response has occurred. Three different families, all strong believers who have adopted many children, have commented that perhaps our family is the one the Lord has in mind for these girls. Because these are people I respect, I'm finding it difficult to shrug off their comments. Would the Lord really want us to adopt these girls?

It's not an easy thing to consider. My husband is a pastor and his salary is even less than he would make as a teacher. My work as Executive Director of Kingdom Kids is very rewarding, but not monetarily. I'm paid a token amount that helps with our food budget. We live pretty frugally but there are definite expenses involved in raising eight children. Just to send five of them to summer camp cost us nearly two months of my salary! Could we possibly stretch our resources to include two more children?

I thoroughly enjoy raising my large family, but a major stress for me is that we can't all ride in one vehicle together. We have a seven passenger van that Steve converted to an eight passenger by purchasing a bench seat at our local junkyard. It worked well until we added Andrew and Dinah to our family. Now we have to drive my very rattly twenty year old car as well as the van wherever we go in order to accommodate a family of ten. In the fall when Peter and Aaron leave for college we will once again all fit into the van. I realize there are worse things than having to drive two vehicles all over town, but truthfully it is frustrating for me. I like our family to be together. If we added two more children to the family we would need to ride in both vehicles year round.

Of course, some well-meaning friends have suggested that we buy a fifteen passenger van. I would love to! But we simply don't have money saved for this and we don't feel it would be wise to go into debt. And even if someone gave us a van we would still need to pay for insurance and maintenance. It's a daunting dilemma.

And what about the workload two more children would add? We're fairly well organized now, but I know that I rely on the older children to help out quite a bit. Would we be pushing the other kids too far if we asked them to stretch even further?

And what of my long-suffering husband? He loves our children dearly, but probably wouldn't have ended up with such a large family had I not been so persistent. Would two more children be two too many?

And truthfully, what of me? In addition to raising our family I spend many hours each week working for Kingdom Kids, and I am quite involved helping Steve with his programs in Children and Family Ministries at church. Would it simply be too much?

And yet, and yet . . . . There is a continuous tug on my heart about this situation. Susannah and I found the girls very appealing, and I desperately want them to be in a Christian family, well-loved and cared for. "Why not ours?" my heart whispers at the most inconvenient times, when I really should be thinking about something else.

Is it possible, because things have gone so well for us regarding our adoptions up to this point, that the Lord is asking us to do something that would require us to trust Him in ways that we haven't had to before? So much of what we've done up to now we've been able to do in our own strength. Yes, there have been challenges, but nothing we haven't been able to resolve fairly easily.

In Hebrews 5:8 we are told, "Although He was a Son, He learned obedience from the things which He suffered." In fifty years or ten years or maybe tomorrow I'll be rejoicing in the presence of the Lord, experiencing things that "eye has not seen and ear has not heard, and which have not entered the heart of man, all that God has prepared for those who love Him" (I Corinthians 2:9). I look forward to this with great anticipation. But once I am with the Lord I will no longer have the opportunity to learn the things He wants me to learn here. My chance to learn obedience through suffering will be over. There will be no more opportunities to be conformed to the image of His Son (Romans 8:29).

I don't want to tell the Lord no if He is asking me to do something. When I was a student at Multnomah Bible College, I asked my New Testament Greek professor, Ed Goodrick, to sum up living the Christian life in a way that would be easy to remember. After a brief pause, he stated, "Trust and obey." We are to trust the Lord for the things we don't understand and obey Him in the things we do understand. This has helped me a great deal in the twenty-five years since Bible school days. I want to trust my God and be an obedient child of His.

But could He possibly ask us to do something that would require taking risks in so many areas? John Piper, in *Don't Waste Your Life*, states "The bottom-line comfort and assurance in all our risk-taking for Christ is that nothing will ever separate us from the love of Christ. Paul asks, 'Shall tribulation, or distress, or persecution, or famine, or nakedness, or danger, or sword separate us from the love of Christ?' (Romans 8:35). His answer is NO! In other words, no misery that a true Christian ever experiences is evidence that he has been cut off from the love of Christ. The love of Christ triumphs over all misery. Romans 8:38–39 makes this crystal-clear: 'For I am sure that neither death nor life, nor angels nor rulers, nor things present nor things to come, nor powers, nor height nor depth, nor anything else in all creation, will be able to separate us from the love of God in Christ Jesus our Lord.'

"On the far side of every risk—even if it results in death—the love of God triumphs. This is the faith that frees us to risk for the cause of God. It is not heroism, or lust for adventure, or courageous self-reliance, or efforts to earn God's favor. It is childlike faith in the triumph of God's love—that on the other side of all our risks, for the sake of righteousness, God will still be holding us. We will be eternally satisfied in Him. Nothing will have been wasted." (1)

So yes, I think that He could ask us to consider all the opposing arguments I listed above and still say yes to His direction.

And therein lies the question. How would I know the Lord is directing us to expand our family yet again, and that it isn't some misguided wish of my conscience working overtime? And isn't there a point when enough is enough?

There are three markers that are giving peace to my heart. First, I know that Steve and I need to be in agreement about any decision we make. If the Lord isn't speaking to Steve about this, even after I lay it all out to him, I think I can be fairly certain His intention is not for us to adopt the children.

Second, if someone shows an interest as I continue to make the girls' needs known to large groups of people, I will know the Lord used me to advocate for them but not to parent them.

Finally, if I follow the suggestion I made earlier and wait six months before pursuing another adoption, I still have three months before I would make a commitment to these girls. The Lord can do many things in that time period to confirm His direction or to change my heart.

I share this personal story to help you think through what the Lord may be asking you to do. Perhaps you face some of the same obstacles that we do and feel discouraged. The Lord may be asking you to trust Him in a way that you never have before. As you consider His plan for your family think about the impact your decision will have on eternity. Our lives on earth are over in a heartbeat. A thousand years from now we'll be experiencing joy we can't even imagine now.

Let's pray for each other as we seek to trust and obey.

Notes:

1. John Piper, *Don't Waste Your Life* (Wheaton, Ill: Crossway Books, 2003), 95.

Conclusion

We've looked at a lot of issues as we seek to make wise decisions and gently guide our adopted children. We'll make mistakes, we'll have all kinds of fun, and maybe sometimes we'll look back, just for a moment, at life before parenthood. Because parenthood is really what we're talking about. Our children are, first and last, our children. The fact that they were adopted adds some interesting ingredients to the mix, but it's not the most important factor in our relationship with our children.

This is your child! The Lord has given you the tremendous privilege and responsibility of preparing this child for adulthood and for eternity. What could be more satisfying and scary at the same time?

The Lord has shown in the past that His promises will be fulfilled. None of His promises fail. He is worthy of our trust and obedience. (Joshua 23:14 NIV)

May you delight in the adventure to which the Lord has called you.

Appendix

Kingdom Kids Adoption Ministries exists to encourage, educate and equip families as they consider adoption. We offer the following:

1) *We present large adoption conferences around the country. Adoption agencies are invited, keynote speakers and multi-media presentations fill whole group sessions, and we offer numerous workshops on pre— and post-adoption topics. We also present a smaller version of these conferences to individual churches. Those interested in sponsoring or attending a conference may contact Kingdom Kids for further information.*

2) *We help families with fund-raising and grants for adoption. We believe there are many people who don't intend to adopt but are willing to make adoption possible for another family. We help potential adoptive*

families contact friends and relatives and encourage them to make a donation which can be used to help pay adoption expenses.

3) *We write adoption resources from a Christian perspective. A current list of resources may be found on our website.*

To order additional copies of

Have your credit card ready and call:

1-877-421-READ (7323)

or please visit our web site at
www.pleasantword.com

Also available at: www.amazon.com

CPSIA information can be obtained at www.ICGtesting.com
Printed in the USA
266436BV00001B/31/A